GOD OF PROMISE

GOD OF PROMISE

INTRODUCING COVENANT THEOLOGY

MICHAEL HORTON

BakerBooks
Grand Rapids, Michigan

© 2006 by Michael Horton

Published by Baker Books
a division of Baker Publishing Group
P.O. Box 6287, Grand Rapids, MI 49516-6287
www.bakerbooks.com

Printed in the United States of America

Library of Congress Cataloging-in-Publication Data
Horton, Michael Scott.
    God of promise : introducing covenant theology / Michael Horton.
        p.   cm.
    Includes bibliographical references.
    ISBN 0-8010-1289-9 (cloth)
    1. Covenant theology. I. Title.
BT155.H77 2006
231.7'6—dc22   2005029887

Italics in biblical quotations indicates emphasis added by the author.

To my teachers, colleagues, and students at Westminster Seminary California, for exhibiting for me the richness of covenant theology for faith and life.

Contents

Acknowledgments

IN ADDITION TO the Reformed tradition more generally (and the fresh examination of that tradition by Richard Muller and many others), I am especially indebted to the work of Geerhardus Vos, Herman Ridderbos, Louis Berkhof, and Meredith G. Kline. As the dedication suggests, this book is the outcome of years as a student of the likes of Robert B. Strimple, W. Robert Godfrey, Dennis Johnson, Mark Futato, and, of course, Meredith Kline. I am also grateful to those from whom I learned so much at Oxford (especially Alister McGrath, who supervised my thesis on a major figure in English Reformed scholasticism) and in my two post-doctoral years at Yale. Yet, now as a professor at my alma mater, I owe special gratitude to my colleagues who constantly refine my thinking and model remarkable churchmanship and pastoral practice along with it. Thanks especially to Bryan Estelle, who took the time to go through the manuscript in painstaking detail, whose suggestions spared me (and my readers) from several mistakes. As for the students, they routinely challenge me almost as much as my colleagues to greater faithfulness to the task of training servants for that enormously weighty calling that we share together in Christ's body. I am grateful also to Paul Brinkerhoff and Don Stephenson at Baker Books for their interest in this project and attention to detail. Finally, thanks to Lisa and those four children of the covenant who remind me daily of the practical implications of trusting the God of Promise.

1

The Big Idea?

WE LIVE IN a world of broken promises. A fragile web of truthful communication and practical commitments connect us to one another, and when any part of that web comes under significant stress, the trust on which our relationships depend can easily break. Self-interest—that is, outright violation of our commitments ("what we have done," in the prayer of confession)—isn't all that tugs on this web; often the pursuit of things that are in themselves worthy but subordinate goods ("what we have left undone") tug on it as well. Either way, we transgress the law of love.

As Jesus reminds us, there is an inseparable connection between the "two tables" of the Law: love of God (the vertical dimension) and love of neighbor (the horizontal). In the fall of humanity in Adam, recapitulated in the history of Israel, human relationships fray as a result of prior infidelity to their covenant Lord. Yet before, during, and after humankind's broken promises, the promise-making and promise-keeping God is present and will not let the web fall apart.

God's very existence is covenantal: Father, Son, and Holy Spirit live in unceasing devotion to each other, reaching outward beyond the Godhead to create a community of creatures serving as a giant analogy of the Godhead's relationship. Created in the image of the Triune God, we are by nature outgoing, interdependent relationship establishers, finding ourselves in the other and not just in ourselves. Unlike the persons of the Trinity, we at one time did not exist. But when God did decide to create, his decree was not that of a lonely monarch, but of a delighted Father, Son, and Holy Spirit establishing a creaturely, finite analogy of their eternal giving and receiving relationship. We were not just created and then *given* a covenant; we were created *as* covenant creatures—partners not in deity, to be sure, but in the drama that was about to unfold in history. As covenant creatures by nature, every person has a relationship with God. What exactly the nature of that relationship happens to be after the fall will be taken up at some length in this book, but there can be no doubt: everyone has a relationship with God, and that relationship is covenantal. Since that is true, it stands to reason that we would want to know more about the nature of that relationship.

So what exactly is a covenant? Anticipating the definition in the next chapter, we can start by saying that from the most commonly used Hebrew word for this concept (*berit*), a covenant is a relationship of "oaths and bonds" and involves mutual, though not necessarily equal, commitments. As we will see shortly, some biblical covenants are unilaterally imposed commands and promises; others are entered into jointly. Some are conditional and others are unconditional. In other words, under the overarching concept of oaths and bonds we encounter a substantial variety of covenants in Scripture.

How remarkable it is that a great God would stoop not only to create finite analogies of himself, but that he would condescend still further to establish a partnership with them, commissioning them to exercise his own righteous and generous reign over the rest of creation.

My goal for this brief survey is to show the richness of this covenantal web and its centrality to the organization of the Bible's diverse teaching. "Reformed theology is simply covenant theology," according to I. John Hesselink. In other words, Reformed theology is guided by a concern to relate various biblical teachings to the concrete covenants in Scripture as their proper context. But is that the usual perception today? People readily associate "Reformed" (i.e., Calvinistic) theology with the so-called Five Points of Calvinism, with its famous TULIP acronym (total depravity, unconditional election, limited atonement, irresistible grace, perseverance of the saints). Encountering the God of sovereign grace is one of the most life-changing experiences in the Christian life, but it is only the beginning of what Reformed theology is all about. While some friends and critics of Reformed theology have reduced Calvinism to "five points," or further still, to predestination, the actual confessions, catechisms, and standard doctrinal works of the Reformed tradition all testify to a far richer, deeper, and all-embracing faith in the God of the covenant. *Reformed* theology is synonymous with *covenant* theology.

The last century of scholarship has helped to strengthen the traditional Reformed homage to the covenantal motif. In the mid-twentieth century, George E. Mendenhall, consolidating a number of studies by others, demonstrated the remarkable parallels between the Hebrew Scriptures (i.e., Old Testament) and ancient Near Eastern (i.e., secular) treaties. "The names given to the two parts of the Bible in Christian tradition rest on the religious conception that the relationship between God and man is established by a covenant."[1]

Although secular scholars also have their own presuppositions and biases, it is unlikely that the recent consensus on the significance of covenant in the Scriptures is the result of a commitment to a central doctrine. One hobby of theologians is to pick out a central teaching in a given religion or theological system by which all of its doctrines and practices can be understood. So, for example, it is said that Rome begins with the doctrine of the church and deduces everything else from it; Lutherans do the same with justification, and Calvinists treat predestination and the sovereignty of God in that manner.

The impression is therefore given that a systematic theology is imposed externally on the biblical text, not allowing Scripture to speak for itself. That this has happened sometimes in Reformed as in other traditions is no doubt true. However, this whole approach to defining core beliefs has come under great suspicion for very good reasons in our day. It reduces a complex network of interrelated themes to a single dogma from which everything is logically made to follow. Although one can find some examples of this simplistic approach in Reformed circles, which always gives rise to various factions of those committed to this or that emphasis, one is hard-pressed to find much resemblance here to the mature development of Reformed theology in its most representative statements.

For example, while divine election is a crucial doctrine in Reformed theology, it is treated in the confessions and catechisms as an important doctrine alongside others. And it certainly never functions as a central dogma from which everything else can be deduced logically. Rather, it is articulated and defended within a web of associated beliefs, all of which are supported by careful exegesis (interpretation of the Scriptures).

So if predestination is not the "central core" of Reformed theology, what is? As a growing body of theologians is demonstrating these days, there is no such dogma. Reformed theology at least attempts to interpret the whole counsel of God in view of the principle that Scripture interprets Scripture. In other words, that which is clearest and is treated with the greatest significance in Scripture interprets those passages that are more difficult and less central to the biblical message. At least the *goal* is to say what Scripture says and to emphasize what Scripture emphasizes. If Scripture itself coalesces around the revelation of Christ as the fulfillment of the Father's plan of redemption, as Jesus himself said, then we are hardly imposing our own nonbiblical theological grid on Scripture in saying that Scripture is centrally a witness to Christ. But we do not begin with a conception of Christ that we have already formed independently of Scripture, by which we judge the Scriptures (deductively); instead, we come to learn from the Scriptures (inductively) that Christ stands at their center.

Yet "Christ" would himself be an abstract idea or concept apart from the biblical doctrine of the Triune God or the Bible's teaching concerning humanity and the history of creation, fall, redemption, and consummation.

So what brings all of these themes together? What unites them is not itself a central dogma but an architectonic structure, a matrix of beams and pillars that hold together the structure of biblical faith and practice. That particular architectural structure that we believe the Scriptures themselves to yield is the covenant. It is not simply the concept of the covenant, but the concrete existence of God's covenantal dealings in our history that provides the context within which we recognize the unity of Scripture amid its remarkable variety.

According to Meredith G. Kline, "It will emerge, we believe, that for purposes of reappraising the Old Testament canon, the most significant development in the last quarter-century has not been the Dead Sea scroll finds but discoveries made concerning the covenants of the Old Testament in the light of ancient Near Eastern treaty diplomacy."[2] Of all the various forms of literature in the Bible, the treaty is the most basic.[3] Old Testament historical records "are extensions of the treaty prologues . . . linked to both law and prophecy, and on both scores served as an instrument of covenant administration."[4] In fact, Kline argues, there is "an architectural aspect to the Bible. . . . In this connection the imagery of God's 'house' comes to the fore in the book of Exodus. That house is built by means of the canonical Scripture which proceeds from the victorious Yahweh."[5]

Like the architecture of most buildings, the framework is largely hidden from view. To be sure, it is visible enough to distinguish one style from another. We can discern the difference between a neoclassical façade and a Victorian house even though we may not

have the terminology down. However, in most buildings at least, one rarely notices the intricate fabric of steel and concrete behind the walls. The same is true in Reformed theology. The covenant is the framework, but it is far from a central dogma. The various covenants are visible and significant, in some "rooms" (i.e., topics) more than others. The covenant of redemption is prominent in discussion of the Trinity, Christ as mediator, and election, while the covenant of creation is more obvious when we talk about God's relationship to the world (especially humanity), and the covenant of grace is most visible when we take up the topics of salvation and the church. However, whenever Reformed theologians attempt to explore and explain the riches of Scripture, they are always thinking *covenantally* about every topic they take up.

So what are the benefits of such an approach?

What Difference Does It Make?

First, as I hope to make clear in the opening chapters, this covenantal structure can be seen to arise naturally from the ordinary reading of the Scriptures from Genesis to Revelation. When we start with a central dogma, we can easily pillage the Scriptures for it and then discard them, no longer needing the Scriptures themselves, but merely logical deduction, to establish everything else as a consequence. How often have we heard important debates about biblical teaching dismissed with a shrug and the words, "You have your verses and we have our verses," as if the Bible itself were internally inconsistent or contradictory? For Christians all of the verses are "our verses." Our interpretation of a given point must be demonstrated not only as taught in this or that passage, but as consistent with the whole teaching of Scripture. Scripture is internally consistent, not contradictory, but we do not always know how to resolve complicated questions that arise from its diverse teaching. We need to have a framework that Scripture itself provides us; otherwise we will serve the whim of our own assumptions about what should or should not be true, given our starting point. As the first chapters unfold, it is hoped that the reader will gain a fresh sense of wonder at this covenantal unity that undergirds the diversity in Scripture.

Second, recognizing the covenantal framework of Scripture unifies what otherwise is too often divided or confused in our day. For example, in a lot of academic theology as well as popular piety, God and creation are either separated or confused. In other words, God is viewed as so completely beyond us that we cannot really know him or have a personal relationship with him. People don't know how to relate God to the world he has made. Some banish God from his own domain, as in deism, in which adherents acknowledge God's existence but deny his personal involvement in the world. God is thus often perceived as an impersonal force or abstract principle. Others simply identify God with the world, as if the difference between God and humans were merely quantitative (God as greater, larger, more impressive, intelligent, and powerful) rather than qualitative (different from that which he has made). Ironically, in either case, God is rendered irrelevant: either by being too distant from us or by being absorbed into us—our will, our intellect, our emotions, our experience. The point of idolatry is to maintain our own autonomy (i.e., sovereignty) over God, either by banishment or absorption. In the one case, we ignore the reality of God; in the other, we use God as a projection for our own felt needs and make him serve our own ends. As we will see, the biblical understanding of God's relationship to the world as covenantal is both a *bridge* that deism ignores and a *bar* to any confusion of the Creator with his creation.

Covenant theology also speaks of the unity of the human and nonhuman creation without simply erasing the difference. In our age, a lot of harm has been done to the natural creation because of the pretensions of human sovereignty. Whereas the covenant of creation places humanity in a privileged position in order to conserve and shepherd the rest of God's creatures for his glory and their good ends, our atheistic culture knows of no obligation to a sovereign God that stands over our own ambitions and drives. At the same time, recognizing humanity's poor stewardship of creation, many of our neighbors today confuse humanity with the nonhuman world just as they collapse the Creator into his creation in an effort to ground ethical responsibility in a divine creation instead of a divine Lord of creation. Covenant theology speaks to this crisis quite definitely.

Further, we see on all hands a tendency to either separate or confuse the individual and the community. On one hand, a rampant Western individualism has unleashed a war of all against all. The individual self is sovereign. This has infected the church profoundly, in both its faith and practice, wherever the emphasis on "me and my personal relationship with God" has supplanted the biblical assumption of covenantal solidarity. Covenant theology, in fact, requires such solidarity: that of the Father, Son, and Holy Spirit in the covenant of redemption; our solidarity with all of creation and especially our being "in Adam" by virtue of the creation covenant and "in Christ" in the covenant of grace.

Significantly, nearly all of the emphasis in Scripture in this regard falls on metaphors of solidarity: the people of God, the holy nation, the congregation, the body with its head and various parts, the vine and its branches, living stones being built into a spiritual temple, a family, and so on. Yet many Christians today are tempted to overreact to individualism by emphasizing the corporate aspect to a degree that seriously downplays the importance Scripture attributes to the personal relationship to God that must be accepted and acted upon by each individual within the covenant. How do we bring the individual and corporate aspects of our theology and practice together in the face of such circumstances? Only, I will argue, by recovering not a concept or an idea, but a concrete covenantal context and practice within which the self is no longer sovereign and self-enclosed *or* lost in the crowd of the "community," but liberated to belong to God and to each other.

Related to all of the preceding is the opposition between body and soul that one often encounters in popular piety. Salvation is often conceived of in terms of being freed from this world and going to another world that is superior in that it is spiritual rather than physical. This concept, however, is far from the biblical understanding of salvation, which confesses its faith in the resurrection of the body and the life to come—not apart from our bodies and the physical creation all around us, but with both! This is the good news that Paul announces in Romans 8:18–24: we are only fully saved when our bodies are raised and the whole creation joins us in its liberation from the effects of the fall.

Much of Christian faith and practice has also tended either to divorce the kingdom of God from or confuse it with the kingdoms of this world. Divorcing the kingdom of God from the kingdoms of this world is accomplished by failing to recognize that all of creation, especially all humans, stand already in a relationship to God as creator and judge in the covenant of creation. We all are bound together ethically in mutual responsibility. Each person, Christian or not, bears God's image, and we can work side by side with non-Christians to fulfill the scriptural command to show love to our neighbors. We must therefore take this world seriously, because we share with non-Christians that image of God and participate with them in ordinary secular callings and cultural endeavors. At the same time, the fall in Eden marks the breaking of this covenant, and since then humanity has developed along two distinct lines: those who build cities and those who call on the name of the Lord (Gen. 4:17–26). Those two lines intersect in the individual Christian, who is a citizen of both kingdoms. But the two kingdoms are distinct. The covenant of creation is not the same as the covenant of grace, and the world is not the church. The kingdom of God does not advance through cultural achievement but through divine rescue. Covenant theology marvelously unites these crucial commitments without confusing them.

Still another benefit of the covenantal grid is the way in which it gives proper place to doctrinal and practical concerns without simply surrendering one to the other. I have found covenant theology particularly enriching when it comes to the frequent warfare between faith and practice—in other words, that all too common debate between doctrine and life or "head knowledge" and "heart knowledge," knowing and doing. In the covenantal thinking we find in Scripture, there is no such thing as true knowledge without love and obedience. To know God is actually, in the Hebrew language, to *acknowledge* God—that is, to walk after God in the way that a servant walked behind a king in a solemn procession, recognizing his sovereignty. One of the rich biblical terms here is *hesed,* or "covenant loyalty." Because such a theology does not arise out of abstract concepts and supposedly universal principles, but out of the historical fact of an actual covenant constitution, it is simultaneously theoretical and practical. The very context of covenant theology is practical: a concrete community life framed, criticized, normed, and corrected by a divinely prescribed pattern of existence.

Related to this is the concern to relate justification and sanctification. In our day, as in others, the truth that we are declared right before God on the basis of someone else's "covenantal loyalty" (*hesed*)—namely, Christ's—is under attack. Covenant theology sees the justification of the individual before God and the justification of God in the great trial of history as two sides of the same coin. It also sees God's declaration in justification as crucially related to this verdict's effect in the new birth, sanctification, and finally, glorification. With its distinction between God's "command" and "promise," the conditional type of covenant God made with humanity in Adam and at Sinai and the unconditional oath he made to the eternal Son, to Adam and Eve after the fall, to Abraham, David, and now to us in Christ, covenant theology is able to articulate the subtle but important nuances that we find in Scripture. It does this without either divorcing law from gospel or confusing them.

Similarly, covenant theology provides a broader biblical context for relating divine and human agency. A covenant involves two parties, so if we begin with the covenant rather than with abstract philosophical questions, the whole discussion changes significantly. It is often supposed that Calvinism highlights a set of biblical passages on God's sovereignty, while Arminians emphasize other passages that teach human responsibility. Thus, this rivalry is simply the consequence of not teaching both with the correct scriptural balance. There certainly is a hyper-Calvinism that fits this description, preoccupied with a distorted concept of God's sovereignty that then pushes everything else to the periphery. Here we do encounter that deductive approach of a central dogma criticized above. But hyper-Calvinism is not Calvinism. When Reformed theology hears Scripture teaching both divine sovereignty and human responsibility, divine election and the universal offer of the gospel, it affirms both even though it confesses that it does not know quite how God coordinates them behind the scenes.

But Arminianism, like hyper-Calvinism, seems to begin with an all-controlling presupposition from which it deduces the possible interpretations of Scripture. That central dogma appears to be a certain libertarian concept of human freedom according to which human responsibility requires a will that is not only free of external coercion, but free of the preferences and character of the willing agent.

When we read all of these passages on divine sovereignty and human responsibility within the context of the covenant and its historical unfolding, however, abstract and speculative questions are exchanged for concrete and historical ones. God does not limit his sovereignty, or any of his other attributes, to make space for human freedom. Rather, his freedom is the very space within which our creaturely freedom is possible (Acts 17:24–28). But neither is God a capricious despot who exercises arbitrary power. Instead, he condescends not only to create, but to bind himself to his creation in the form of covenants.

By articulating its view of God's sovereignty within the context of Triune love in eternity (the covenant of redemption), solidarity with all that he has made (the covenant of creation), and his saving purposes in Christ and by his Spirit (the covenant of grace), covenant theology is able to give proper place not only to "pro-sovereignty" verses in Scripture, but to those passages that empha-size also the significance of human action. In the covenant, both the Lord and the Servant are on trial for their faithfulness: there simply can be no choice between whose action we take seriously. This focus curbs our speculative tendencies. Not by probing God's secret counsels in eternity, but by concentrating on the historical unfolding of his covenants with us do we come to know that we are heirs in Christ. Doing so keeps our feet on the ground.

Covenant theology also helps us to read the Old and New Testaments together without confusing them. Many of us were raised in churches where we only rarely came into contact with the Old Testament, and even then it was usually in the form of Bible stories in which some moral trait could be held up to us for our emulation. But many Christians are not quite sure what to do with that part of their Bible. Does Scripture read as one book from Genesis to Revelation? Is there one plot? And related to this, one people? Or does the Old Testament give us one plan of salva-tion for one people (Israel) while the New Testament gives us a different plan of salvation for a different people (the church)?

Covenant theology begins with continuity rather than discon-tinuity, not because of any a priori bias, but because Scripture itself moves from promise to fulfillment, not from one distinct program to another and then back again. At the same time, cov-enant theology recognizes in Scripture itself a distinction between specific types of covenants. Some demand unswerving obedience as a condition of their fulfillment, such as the covenant made by the people at Sinai.

To read Deuteronomy, for example, as if it were timeless prin-ciples of blessing and cursing is to confuse this covenant concerning a national, geopolitical entity (i.e., the nation of Israel) with the eternal plan of redemption carried forward in the unconditional divine promise to Abraham and fulfilled in Christ. Again, covenant theology helps enormously in understanding both the continuities and discontinuities as we read Scripture. It helps us to see the basic *continuity between* the old and new covenants in terms of a single covenant of grace running throughout, as well as the *discontinuity within* even the Old Testament itself when it comes to the principle of a unilateral divine promise and an arrangement dependent on personal obedience to all that God commands.

Covenant theology can also help us pull together the often ambiguous relationship between Word and sacrament. Throughout the history of God's covenantal dealings, a verbal pronouncement of the covenant, including its blessings and curses, is enacted, sealed, and ratified by public and visible rituals. Today, various Christian traditions are divided between Word-centered and sacrament-centered orientations. Some churches seem at least in practice to assume that we could get along fine without baptism and the Lord's Supper as long as we had preaching (and perhaps a good choir!). Other churches seem—again, in practice if not always in theory—to assume that the real business is the spectacle of the sacrament itself. Instead, we need to reaffirm in our day that preaching and sacrament, verbal renewal of the covenant and visual confirmation of our participation in it, are inseparable. This mutual interdependence of Word and sacrament is best confirmed not by theories about what we think is useful in church, but by appeal to scriptural context in which both arise as the "cutting of a covenant."

Finally, we could mention the cleavage one often feels today between the nurture of the Christian body and its mission to the world. Alongside an emphasis on the covenant community and therefore the intergenerational shape of disciple-making through the public gathering there is the call to extend the family through personal as well as corporate witness.

From Timeless Ideas to Historical Events

As Old Testament scholar Walther Eichrodt argued, "the covenant-union between Yahweh and Israel is an original element in all sources, despite their being in fragmentary form."[6]

From the very beginning, the Israelites regarded themselves as a coalition of tribes committed not to nationalism nor bound by political aims, but "called out" by God to belong to him by means of a covenant. Thus, "God's disclosure of himself is not grasped speculatively, not expounded in the form of a lesson; it is as he breaks in on the life of his people in his dealings with them and moulds them according to his will that he grants them knowledge of his being."[7] The promissory character of this covenant "provides life with a goal and history with a meaning."

> Because of this the fear that constantly haunts the pagan world, the fear of arbitrariness and caprice in the Godhead, is excluded. With this God men know exactly where they stand; an atmosphere of trust and security is created, in which they find both the strength for a willing surrender to the will of God and joyful courage to grapple with the problems of life. . . . In this way history acquires a value which it does not possess in the religions of the ancient civilizations. . . . Their view of the divine activity was too firmly imprisoned in the thought-forms of their Nature-mythology. In Israel, on the other hand, the knowledge of the covenant God and his act of redemption aroused the capacity to understand and to present the historical process, at first only in the limited framework of the national destiny but later also universally, as the effect of a divine will.[8]

It was chiefly the concept of covenant (with its corollary, election) that guarded against a civil religion and made Yahweh's will rather than national aspirations the basis for life.[9] Not only the Old Testament, but the New Testament as well, can be understood only from the perspective of God's covenantal ways.[10]

Indeed, we do live in a world of broken promises and broken dreams. Furthermore, there are lots of "covenants" in the Bible. But is the covenant motif so crucial in Scripture, important enough to be regarded as its architectural structure? And if so, what specific kinds of covenants are definitive here? Answering those two questions will be the purpose of the following chapters.

2

God and Foreign Relations

IF CHAPTER 1 is right in asserting the architectural significance of the covenant motif, then what exactly is the background
for the biblical concept of "covenant"? Once again, it is important
to remind ourselves that we are not treating the covenant motif as
a central doctrine. In other words, it is not a matter of reducing
everything in the Bible to the covenant, but of recognizing the
rich covenantal soil in which every biblical teaching takes root.
In the title of his groundbreaking work *The Treaty of the Great
King*,[1] Meredith Kline characterized not only the content, but the
very form of Scripture. We will first briefly explore this secular
background and then focus our attention on the covenantal warp
and woof of Scripture.

The Bible and International Law

One of the remarkable examples of God's providence is the rise
of the international treaty. This is notable not only because it created the basis for justice and security in a world of rogues, thugs,

and vigilantes resembling characters from TV Westerns, but also because it was to be such a suitable context for the relationship that God would establish with Israel. Before a single word of the Bible was penned, the ancient Near East already had in place a secular version of the covenant in the form of its suzerain-vassal treaties.[2] A suzerain was a great king, like an emperor, while a vassal was what we would today call a "client state." The suzerain-vassal relationship was like that of a feudal knight and his tenants in the Middle Ages, Buckingham Palace and Nairobi or Hong Kong during the era of colonialism, or Moscow and its satellites in the Soviet Union.

George E. Mendenhall's magisterial *Law and Covenant in Israel and the Ancient Near East* highlighted the remarkable parallels between ancient (especially Hittite) treaties and the covenantal structure of Old Testament thought and practice.[3] Ancient Near Eastern scholar Delbert Hillers likewise comments on the similarities. "The term that has become common is 'suzerainty treaty,' and this word from the language of feudalism fits the situation very well."[4] The treaties from the Hittite Empire (1450–1180 BC) are especially similar to what we find in the Bible. In those international pacts, the term "oaths and bonds" is employed.

Let's say that several villages on the outskirts of an empire have banded together to try to form something like a league or confederacy. They may perhaps have enough in the way of resources as means of exchange, and they may be capable of setting up institutions for their common welfare. However, they cannot provide for a standing army beyond a small militia that is hardly sufficient to stave off a sizable band of villains, much less an invading imperial force. So the leader of the confederacy, perhaps himself a king, turns to a great king, usually an emperor with forces in the region large enough to protect the client state. In such a case, the lesser king (vassal) could enter into a covenant with the great king (suzerain), or as often happened, a suzerain could rescue a vassal from impending doom and therefore claim his right to annex the beneficiaries of his kindness by covenant to his empire. They would be his people, and he would be their suzerain. Their own king might continue to rule locally but as a viceroy of the emperor.

What is often present in these ancient treaties and missing in modern analogies is the fact that these were not merely legal contracts but involved the deepest affections. The great king was the father adopting the captives he had liberated from oppression. Consequently, he was not simply to be obeyed externally, but loved; not only feared, but revered; not only known as the legal lord of the realm, but acknowledged openly as the rightful sovereign. Of course, there were good suzerains and bad ones, but there was widespread agreement at least in the ancient Near East that this is what constituted a lawful covenant.

All of this is somewhat difficult for us to grasp, since for most of us, our day-to-day experience is shaped by life in liberal democracies in which personal choice and rights are enshrined. The dominant model in the so-called developed nations of the West is the social contract: each person, though naturally sovereign, surrenders a bit of sovereignty to the state in order to receive certain benefits in return. The state then acts as a sort of proxy for the collective will of the people, conceived largely as individuals. In more cynical versions of this story (especially that of Thomas Hobbes), human beings are naturally at war with each other, and the only thing that will save us from our mutually assured destruction is an all-powerful state. Whatever the character of the states engendered by the ancient Near Eastern treaty, it certainly was not *that*.

What then were the distinguishing features of such a treaty? A century before the conquest of Canaan, the Hittite treaties included several typical elements.[5]

First was the *preamble* ("thus [saith] NN [name], the great king, king of the Hatti land, son of NN ... the valiant"), identifying the one who made the treaty.

The second element was the *historical prologue*. This wasn't just window dressing; it justified everything that followed. Given the history—let's say that the suzerain had rescued the smaller nation from an invading army—what could be expected other than the hearty acceptance of a grateful people? By telling the story of what happened, the suzerain showed that the lesser king was in no bargaining position. The lesser king and his people had been treated mercifully and had no claim upon the great king.

Historical prologues kept treaties firmly planted. As secular treaties, they were nothing like the religious myths the ancients told, for instance, about the creation of the world. The religion of these people was cyclical and mythological, but their politics had a clear historical footing. It is no wonder that when God took up this treaty motif for his relationship to Israel, the utterly historical character shaped the religious as much as the political life of the people. There wasn't an irrational realm of myth on the one hand (religion) and a rational realm of history and politics (everyday life) on the other. Rather, God claimed sovereignty over all of life and anchored this total claim in history rather than in myth or general principles of truth and morality. He said, "I am the LORD your God, who brought you out of the land of Egypt, out of the house of slavery. You shall have no other gods before me" (Exod. 20:2–3). It was because certain things had *happened* that Israel was obligated to him.

A third element of ancient treaties was *stipulations*. We see this in all of the Hittite treaties, as also in the summary of the covenant at Sinai just cited: "I am the one who redeemed you. . . . Therefore, you shall not. . . . You shall. . . ." The stipulations, or terms of the treaty, were set forth. Those who kept the stipulations were covenant-keepers, while those who violated them were covenant-breakers. At this point in the ancient treaties, there was also an appeal to witnesses, which involved calling upon the respective deities. Both sides would call upon the sky-god and sacred mountains and rivers, to witness the oath and testify against either party in the event of transgression.

Again, this was to be a relationship of trust, love, and genuine faithfulness, not simply of external obligation and consent. Far from being arbitrary, merely legal dos and don'ts, the stipulations were an utterly reasonable duty. They fit the character of the liberation these ancient people had experienced. Typically, they involved the following: no backroom alliances with other kings, no murmuring against the suzerain, and payment of an annual tribute tax to the great king. The vassal also had to pledge to raise a regiment to join the suzerain's army in any action taken against a fellow vassal under the suzerain's protection.

Consequently, the stipulations were followed by *sanctions* that spelled out what would happen if the vassal failed to uphold the treaty. Sanctions included the eviction of the people from their homes and land and their exile.

Just as the suzerain graciously and without any inherent obligation pledged to move against those who invaded his vassal territory as if it were his own capital, he would move against the vassal state itself just as ferociously should the terms of the covenant be violated. The sanctions were then followed by the blessings and curses formula. The suzerain's action of calling down the wrath of the witnessing gods should the vassal state prove unfaithful suggests that the assumption was never far off that the gods would be acting in the person of the suzerain and his army. Although the suzerain was in no way obligated prior to the covenant, he pledged himself to guard his vassals. The political term for this was *invocation*. A vassal king in trouble could invoke the suzerain's pledge of rescue. He was authorized to use the great king's name like the lever of a fire alarm: by breaking the glass and pulling the lever, as it were, invoking the name of the suzerain, he could be assured of his lord's swift protection.

A fifth basic element provided for *the deposit of the treaty* tablets in the sacred temples of both parties (again, so the deities of both partners could serve as constant witnesses) as well as *periodic public reading*, so that each new generation clearly understood its obligations.[6]

In addition to the treaty itself was the public ceremony that sealed it and put it into effect. Such ceremonies included an event in which the suzerain and vassal would pass between the halves of slaughtered animals, as if to say, "May the same fate befall me should I fail to keep this covenant." In other rituals, the vassal king would walk behind the great king down an aisle as a sign of loyalty, service, and submission. (Hence, the language of "walking after" God in the Scriptures.) Celebratory meals at which the treaty was ratified were held as well.

An important feature was that the suzerain never took an oath himself. It was his treaty, after all. The stipulations and sanctions (curses and blessings) all fell on the vassal.[7] Whatever the suzerain decided to do by way of self-obligation was done in absolute freedom. Delbert Hillers writes, "The covenant is regularly spoken of as that which the sovereign gave to his vassal—it is the sovereign's covenant. He is the author. The specific obligations imposed upon the vassal are called the 'words' of the sovereign, for to speak is to command when the great king delivers utterance."[8]

One of the running themes in the Bible, however, is that the nations and their armies, their kings and their gods, their chariots and their ivory palaces cannot save but are in truth assembled against the Lord and his anointed king (Psalm 2). Israel was not first of all a nation, but a church, a community called out of darkness, sin, oppression, and evil to form the nucleus of God's worldwide empire. Not only the politics, but the religion, was anchored in historical events that gave rise to faith that this covenant Lord would be faithful to his promises. So there was a basis for confidence. The future was not indeterminate, left to chance or the caprice of the stars, the gods, demons, or natural forces, but was in the hands of a good God who had condescended to take them into covenant. They knew that if they called on the name of this covenant Lord, they would be saved from their enemies. They knew this because the Lord heard their groaning in Egypt and in Babylon and finally answered the cry of his people in the birth of the one who would save them from their sins.

Biblical Covenants

In pagan religions and philosophies, human beings were often seen, at least in their spiritual or intellectual aspect, as a spark of the divine essence. Quite often a particular race was identified with the divinity, and the king was seen as an incarnation of a divine figure. The case was, of course, quite different for Israel. The sovereign God, creator and lord of all, was utterly distinct from his creation. No part of God's nature or knowledge coincided with the creature at any point. That is to say, God is transcendent. Therefore, any relationship that one might have with this God would have to be something other than a *natural* relationship—that is, the relationship could not be explained in terms of, say, a common spiritual essence shared by the Creator and a creature. According to the Bible, that relationship—a covenant—is established by God in his freedom. We are not related to God by virtue of a common aspect of our being, but by virtue of a pact that he himself makes with us to be our God.

In distinction from pagan mythology, the denial of any *natural* connection between the Creator and creature establishes the biblical emphasis on God's *transcendence* (his incomprehensible majesty). However, the fact that God has chosen to enter into a personal relationship with us by means of covenant underscores his *immanence* (or nearness). It is not surprising then that God adapted the international treaty as the template for his relationship to creatures. That relationship really is a matter of "foreign relations." The creature, even the one made in his image, is never divine or semidivine, but is always other than God. Although there may be similarities between the creature and the Creator, there are always greater differences. In other words, God not only differs *quantitatively* (i.e., possessing greater degrees of being, wisdom, omnipotence, etc.) but *qualitatively*. This is why the divine-human relationship is characterized in theology as *analogical* rather than *univocal*. That is, there is no point at which the Creator and his creation overlap with any exact (univocal) identity at any point. At the same time, created in God's image, humankind can be described as an analogy of God: similar but never the same. "Covenant" is exactly the right concept for such "foreign relations."

While the nations believed they were at the whim of gods and forces that could prove arbitrary, caught in a divinized cycle of nature, Israel could be confident that they, and the whole creation, were in the hands of a personal God who could be trusted. Key to this trust was a covenant. Such a bond gave a certain degree of security, an atmosphere of belonging to their God in a reciprocal relationship. God had bound himself to them. Thus, their worldview engendered a history rather than a mythological cycle of nature. Promise and fulfillment, not birth and rebirth—movement forward, not just in circles—gave rise to Israel's confidence. History became important because it was God's theater in which he promised to bring about his purposes for his people and indeed the whole world. Even in their sin and rebellion, Israel could take confidence in the good news of redemption in the future. It was chiefly the concept of covenant (with its corollary, election) that guarded against a civil religion and made Yahweh's will rather than national aspirations the basis for life.[9]

But are the similarities between ancient Near Eastern treaties and biblical covenants no more than superficial? The word for covenant (*berit*) occurs two hundred times in the Old Testament, and even where the technical term is not used, there are instances of covenant-making. Far from engendering a legalistic form of religion, Israel's covenant with Yahweh meant that they were no longer at the whim of petty warlords and heavy-handed suzerains. "The covenant relationship itself may very well be regarded as a guarantee of freedom from every other political suzerainty."[10]

While the basic structure and elements of the covenant in the Old Testament texts bear close resemblances to the Hittite treaties, what distinguishes Israel from all other nations is that their God is the acting suzerain and not merely a witness to a human sovereign's imposition of a relationship. It is this intimacy of the I-you exchange between suzerain and vassal that is transposed into the form of the relationship between Yahweh and Israel. "When the statement is made that religion is based on covenant, it implies that a form of action which originated in legal custom has been transferred to the field of religion."[11]

Beginning with the Law, we will move through the Prophets and the period between the two testaments into the New Testament era in an effort to survey the specific covenant forms that we find in Scripture. Our goal is to move from the particular (inductive) to the general (deductive), that is, from exegesis of particular passages to larger biblical-theological trajectories, leading finally to systematic theology.

We begin with the Law. Not even this part of the Bible, however, can be identified simply with the form of suzerainty treaty I have been describing. Remember, this international treaty was imposed by the suzerain without any inherent obligation assumed by him. It imposed obligations. In other words, it was in the category of what one might call "pure law"—not in any pejorative sense, as if "law" is inherently oppressive. After all, as we have seen, the stipulations (actual laws) were justified by the historical prologue (actual deliverance). However, there was no sense that the vassal was simply to do his best to follow the stipulations, nor any promise that the suzerain would be merciful in case of breach. In biblical terms, a suzerainty treaty is a "Do this and you shall live" kind of arrangement!

The oath that Israel took at the foot of Mount Sinai has clear affinities with the suzerainty treaty. God had delivered them from Egypt and taken them for his people, but now they had to own Yahweh as their covenant Lord. Hearing the terms (stipulations), they replied, "Everything the LORD has said we will do" (Exod. 24:3 NIV). The covenant at Sinai was an oath sworn by the Israelites, just as in the suzerainty treaty. The elements of the treaty form were clearly present: the historical prologue (liberation from Egypt), the stipulations (ten words or commandments), sanctions with the usual blessings and curses formula, with the warning that the Israelites were "but [God's] tenants" (Lev. 25:23 NIV) and were subject to eviction if they violated the covenant.

And in fact, the Law (Torah) itself prophesied that this would happen (Deuteronomy 29).

It is important, however, to distinguish between the law's strictness in relation to individual salvation (demanding an absolute perfection that we cannot fulfill since the fall) and in relation to the national covenant with Israel (requiring an external conformity, with provisions for default). What degree of disobedience God could put up with in order to allow Israel to keep its tenure in his land was always up to God, of course. His patience (long-suffering) receive all too many opportunities to be displayed. Yet the very fact that God does exercise patience in this relationship points up that the Sinai covenant is not simply identical to the pre-fall Adamic covenant. After the fall, a covenant of works arrangement—even for a national covenant rather than individual salvation, cannot really get off the ground if absolutely perfect obedience is the condition. Remember, the purpose of the Jewish theocracy (i.e., the old covenant) was to point forward through types to the coming Messiah. But how could God maintain a typological kingdom that kept the focus of future anticipation on Christ if that kingdom's existence depended at every moment on obedience? If the terms in Canaan were as strictly enforced as they were in Eden, the Israelites would never have even made it to Canaan (as we see in Exodus 32–34, not to mention in their testing of God in the desert).

What was necessary on the nation's part was, as M. G. Kline expresses it, an "appropriate measure of national fidelity."[12] Enough covenantal obedience was necessary to keep the typology legible, serving its purpose of directing attention to the true and lasting kingdom of God that it prefigured. This does not mean that the world only needed a redeemer who could roughly approximate the requirement of perfect obedience. After all, the covenant of works made with Adam and his posterity still requires fulfillment if anyone is to be saved. There must be a second Adam, not just a second Israel. There are both continuities and discontinuities between the covenant of works made with Adam and the republication of the works-covenant at Sinai, differences that are determined largely by changing historical contexts (viz., the fall and God's determination to have a typological system whose every detail was designed to prefigure his Son's arrival in world history).

The Decalogue and Joshua 24 also fit the suzerainty treaty pattern ("Do this and you shall live"), but "it can readily be seen that the covenant with Abraham (and Noah) is of completely different form," notes Mendenhall.

> Both in the narrative of Gen 15 and 17, and in the later references to this covenant, it is clearly stated or implied that it is Yahweh Himself who swears to certain promises to be carried out in the future. It is not often enough seen that no obligations are imposed upon Abraham. Circumcision is not originally an obligation, but a sign of the covenant, like the rainbow in Gen 9. It serves to identify the recipient(s) of the covenant, as well as to give a concrete indication that a covenant exists. It is for the protection of the promisee, perhaps, like the mark on Cain of Gen 4. The covenant of Moses, on the other hand, is almost the exact opposite. It imposes specific obligations upon the tribes or clans without binding Yahweh to specific obligations, though it goes without saying that the covenant relationship itself presupposed the protection and support of Yahweh to Israel.[13]

I will return to this point below in my analysis of the differences between the suzerainty treaty and the royal grant (also known as the patron covenant): the former is conditional, while the latter is an unconditional promise on the part of the suzerain.

As mentioned above, we should not think of Israel in its emergence as a federation of tribes entirely linked by blood. Scripture itself indicates that those who had passed through the Red Sea and now gathered at Sinai were a "mixed multitude" (Num. 11:4 NKJV). Each person, each family, pledged loyalty to the stipulations God issued at Sinai. There was no king to representatively "stand in" for the people; they themselves vowed to keep God's law. The solemn ceremony putting the covenant into effect was twofold, notes Mendenhall: "One ceremony is the sprinkling of blood upon altar and people, another is the banquet in the presence of Yahweh." Furthermore, "The tradition of the deposit of the law in the Ark of the Covenant is certainly connected with the covenant customs of pre-Mosaic times."[14] Given the equation of gossip or untrusting speech or conduct with breach of the covenant stipulations in the Hittite treaty, "The traditions of the 'murmurings' in the wilderness is also a motif which receives new meaning in the light of the covenant."[15]

The covenant of Joshua 24 follows exactly the Hittite features: the author of the covenant identified (v. 2b), historical prologue in I-you form, stipulations, people themselves as witnesses, deposit of covenant in sanctuary and another witness (the great stone).

The covenant form itself

> was the source of the "feeling for history" which is such an enigma in Israelite literature. And perhaps even more important is the fact that what we now call "history" and "law" were bound up into an organic unit from the very beginnings of Israel itself. Since the cultus was at least connected with the covenant proclamation or renewal, we can see that in early Israel, history, cultus, and "law" were inseparable, and that the history of Israelite religion is not the history of the gradual emergence of new theological concepts, but of the separation and re-combination of these three elements so characteristic of Israelite religion, over against the mythological religions of their pagan neighbors.[16]

In the period of the monarchy, Yahweh was the witness in the anointing of the king.[17] But similarities between the Hittite suzerainty treaties and biblical covenants begin to diminish. An interesting feature in the Hebrew covenants is the "everlasting covenant" associated with David and his throne: "In Israel also the term *berit 'olam* occurs only in connection with the dynasty of David until the Exilic period."[18] What has happened? Are there two different covenant traditions? We will take up that question in the next chapter.

3

A Tale of Two Mothers

CHALLENGING HIS OPPONENTS' conviction that salvation not only comes *from* the Jews, but only comes to those
who themselves *become* Jews, Paul, the apostle to the Gentiles,
explains that there are two very different types of covenantal arrangements in the Old Testament itself. Paul speaks forcefully in
Galatians 4 of two covenants, two mountains, and two mothers.
A covenant of law is established at Mount Sinai, engendering an
earthly Jerusalem, which is identified with Hagar the slave; and
a covenant of promise is given to Abraham and his seed, engendering a heavenly Jerusalem, which is identified with Sarah the
free woman. Confusion of these two covenants, Paul believed,
lay at the heart of the Galatian heresy, a charge repeated by the
Protestant Reformers in the sixteenth century.

The principles of law (i.e., personal performance) and promise
(i.e., inheritance of an estate by virtue of the performance of another) give rise to antithetical forms of religion. The inheritance,
Paul insists, is either by our obedience to the law or by someone
else's, bestowed on us by free grace alone; it cannot be by both.
Being the beneficiary of an inheritance is not the same as being

a successful partner who receives a reward for service rendered. Paul makes this point not only in Galatians, but in such places as Romans 3 and 4, where Abraham is once more presented as the paradigm case of justification through faith alone "apart from the deeds of the law" (Rom. 3:28 NKJV), so that the inheritance (election, redemption, new life) may come to Gentiles as well as Jews. Boasting is therefore entirely excluded (3:27). "Now to him who works, the wages are not counted as grace but as debt. But to him who does not work but believes on Him who justifies the ungodly, his faith is accounted for righteousness" (4:4–5 NKJV). Salvation has always come through a covenant of grace (founded on an eternal and unilateral covenant of redemption), rather than on a contract or one's personal fulfillment of the law.

So we have two principles or "laws" at work, which in Galatians 4 Paul actually calls "covenants": a covenant of law, which promises blessing upon perfect obedience and curses for any transgression, and a covenant of promise, which promises blessing as a gift resulting from the personal performance of another. Both covenants have the same goal, promise the same blessings, and threaten the same curses. However, according to one, the blessing is attained by us personally, and in the other, it is bestowed as an inheritance.

Covenant theology can either contribute to the confusion that Paul recognized in Galatia or alleviate it, depending on the specific kind of covenant theology being articulated. In an effort to offer a biblical-theological definition, we have to go back behind Paul's famous allegory of the two mothers and try to discern the Old Testament background. While there are certainly more than two explicit covenants in Scripture, they can all be grouped around two *kinds* of arrangements: conditional covenants that impose obligations and unconditional covenants that announce a divine promise. I will attempt to show the importance of distinguishing these two types for interpreting the biblical message.

Already by the conclusion of the last chapter we were beginning to see that not all biblical covenants fit the suzerainty treaty pattern. Can there be more than one type of biblical covenant? If so, how would the other differ from this suzerainty structure that we see so clearly evident at Sinai and in Joshua 24? Too often in the last two centuries scholars have attempted to squeeze all the data into one definition. As Delbert Hillers remarks, "It is not the case of six blind men and the elephant, but of a group of learned paleontologists creating different monsters from the fossils of six separate species."[1] Even when we are talking about Israel in the Old Testament, it is not enough to talk about *the* covenant, as if there were only one covenantal arrangement that could account for all of the conditional and unconditional language. We will first look at the precise nature of the Sinai covenant (a covenant of law) and then the Abrahamic covenant (a covenant of promise).

Father Moses, Mother Hagar

Jewish readers of Paul's allegory in Galatians 4 may well have thought he was uninformed. Everyone who had paid any attention in Sabbath lessons would have known that Sarah was the mother of Isaac (and therefore of the Jews), while Hagar was the mother of Ishmael (and therefore of the people we would call Arabs today). Furthermore, Mount Sinai was the house of freedom, as determinative of Jewish identity as the Declaration of Independence is for Americans. Was Paul confused about the fundamental details of his own people's history? It is not very likely, since he was a highly trained scribe in the most esteemed tradition of Pharisees.

Moreover, earlier Jesus had raised the ire of the religious leaders by informing them that they were not children of Abraham simply by virtue of their physical lineage (John 8:39–59). It was their response to *him* that demonstrated whether they were truly Abraham's heirs.

Paul was not confused. Throughout Galatians he makes the case that the covenant of law (i.e., the Sinaitic covenant with its ceremonial and civil legislation for life in Canaan) is different from the covenant of promise (i.e., the Abrahamic covenant with its promise of a seed through whom all the nations of the earth would be blessed). Paul is saying here that the former covenant concerned earthly, temporary measures that served as types of the heavenly, eternal reality promised and confirmed in the latter covenant. The earlier (Abrahamic) covenant cannot be annulled by the later (Mosaic) covenant, he insists. Those who seek to be justified by law are under the curse (i.e., sanctions) of that law, because this covenant does not grade on a curve but requires absolute, perfect, personal obedience to everything in it.

Only earthly, temporal blessings can be attained by means of an earthly, temporal covenant, and Israel has demonstrated that they are no better able than the rest of the human race even to remain in that typological land by their own fidelity. Again, to emphasize this, the absolute, personal, perfect obedience to God's law is the measure for acceptance in the covenant of works that God made with all of humanity in Adam. That is the standard with which Paul is working here: not merely the external, general obedience to the commands (circumcision, dietary laws, the Decalogue, observing the holy days, and so forth), which sufficed as appropriate obedience to maintain the theocracy, but the inward love of God and neighbor that God required of humanity originally in creation. As Paul's critics had confused the principles of law and promise, they had also confused the *relative* fidelity required in the *national* covenant and thus they *remain in the typological land* with the *absolute* faithfulness required of *every person* in order to fulfill all righteousness and thus appear safely in God's *heavenly* presence. The Abrahamic covenant leads to Christ and thus the heavenly realities of everlasting liberty; the Sinaitic covenant was a "schoolmaster" (Gal. 3:24 KJV) leading to Christ by types and shadows and by showing that we could not keep it. All who seek to be justified by it no longer seek salvation as Abraham's heirs. The tables are now turned: the very people who seek the closest affinity to Moses and Sinai end up missing the fulfillment of the *prior* covenant of promise in the seed who is received through faith alone.

Paul's argument can be easily justified by its Old Testament background. Exodus 20, where we discover the giving of the Ten Commandments at Sinai, bears the marks of a suzerainty treaty. Hillers points out:

> Note that there is no formal obligation on Yahweh's part [in Exod. 20], just as the Hittite king did not swear to perform anything in a treaty with a vassal. Yahweh's good will is implicit; he is the one who has graciously brought them out of the house of bondage. He will continue to be loyal and kind, since he is "One who keeps faith unto thousands of generations, with those who love me and keep my commandments." But he swears nothing.[2]

Many examples of the blessings and curses formula can be found in Scripture, especially in Leviticus 26 and Deuteronomy 28. In fact, Deuteronomy is itself the Sinai covenant in summary form. Indeed, says Hillers, "the whole book is a covenant on a grand scale, with historical introduction, stipulations, and the closing blessings and curses in chapter 28."[3] Then there is the blood of the covenant sprinkled on the people, after which Moses and the seventy elders (with Aaron and his sons) go up to share a meal with God.

Joshua 24 evidences the same suzerainty treaty pattern. First, in chapter 8 we read, "Afterward, Joshua read all the words of the law—the blessings and the curses—just as it is written in the Book of the Law" (v. 34 NIV). Here, in fact, the principle of personal performance is so emphasized that the people themselves are the witnesses for and against themselves. If they obey, they will be blessed and confirmed in the land. If they disobey, they will be cursed and driven from the land.

Unlike Exodus 20, here in Joshua 24 the narrative prologue goes all the way back to Abraham. However, what is striking is that it nevertheless retains the suzerainty treaty form: "Choose this day whom you will serve" (v. 15). Each family had to accept the covenant for itself, unlike the Hittite treaties that were made with the head of state. The emphasis on personal performance of the covenant conditions could not be stronger. And in each of these examples of Israel's national covenant with God, the elements of the suzerainty treaty are in place: historical prologue, stipulations, sanctions, followed by the blessings and curses formula, sacrifice, and a ritual meal. The principle is clear: "Do this and you shall live." And the response of Israel is just as obvious: "All this we will do." This is a covenant of personal obligation requiring the oath-taker to fulfill all the terms and conditions or suffer the consequences. Now we move backward in time, to the prior covenant made with Abraham.

Father Abraham, Mother Sarah

Just how different are the Abrahamic and Sinaitic covenants? Perhaps the most important source for the former is Genesis 15. The ancient Near Eastern treaties involved a number of ceremonies for making a pact, and we find many of these carried over into Israel's practice as well. "The most widely attested form of swearing to a covenant, however, involved cutting up an animal," notes Hillers.

> The man taking the oath is identified with the slaughtered animal. "Just as this calf is cut up, so may Matiel be cut up," is the way it is put in the text of an Aramaic treaty from the eighth century BC, and an earlier document describes a similar ceremony: "Abba-An swore to Yarim-Lim the oath of the gods, and cut the neck of a lamb, (saying): 'If I take back what I gave you....'" Among the Israelites it seems that a common way of identifying the parties was to cut up the animal and pass between the parts. [See Jer. 34:18.] From this ceremony is derived the Hebrew idiom for making a treaty, *karat berit*, "to cut a treaty."[4]

Homer uses the same idiom: *horkia tamnein,* "to cut oaths."[5]
The phrase "to cut a covenant" is used as early as 1400 BC in
Aramaic and Phoenician as well as Hebrew records.[6] That shows
how closely identified were the cutting ritual (and the consequent
shedding of blood) and the enactment of the covenant. The covenant *was* the cutting and vice versa.

Given this background, the otherwise strange ritual in Genesis
15 makes a lot of sense. Typical of a suzerain bestowing a royal gift
on his loyal vassal, Yahweh tells Abram, "I am your shield, your
very great reward" (v. 1 NIV). God is both the defender against
hostile forces and the benefactor who will ensure an inheritance
for the future. Abram protests on the basis of the obvious state
of affairs: no heir and therefore no future. While he attempts
to grasp his future by his own personal performance (through
Hagar), Yahweh assures him that his inheritance will come only
through his own promise (through Sarah). In verses 7–11, this
promise is sealed in a vision of one of those ancient Near Eastern
cutting ceremonies ratifying a treaty. In this case, however, the
covenanting parties are not walking together between the severed
halves. Instead, God alone takes that walk, assuming all of the
responsibility for carrying the promise through to the end and
bearing all of the curses for its breach. It is a one-sided promise.

Scholars of ancient Near Eastern texts see in Genesis 15 a classic
example of a royal grant as opposed to a suzerainty treaty. Royal
grants were "an outright gift by a king to a subject. . . . A typical
brief example runs as follows: 'From this day forward Niqmaddu
son of Ammistamru king of Ugarit has taken the house of Pabeya
[. . .] which is in Ullami, and given it to Nuriyana and to his descendants forever. Let no one take it from the hand of Nuriyana
or his descendants forever. Seal of the king.'"[7] But there are no
ancient Near Eastern equivalents of the self-maledictory oath
(i.e., calling down curses upon oneself) as a royal grant. It is as
if, from the divine side, the covenant made with Abraham is a
suzerainty treaty in which God swears unilaterally to personally
perform all of the conditions and suffer all of the curses for its

violation, but from the human side, the same covenant is a royal grant, an inheritance bestowed freely and in utter graciousness on the basis of the Great King's performance.

The Abrahamic covenant is a lot like the Noahic covenant. Neither includes a historical prologue or stipulations (i.e., obligations imposed on the servant of the covenant), and therefore neither looks very much like a suzerainty treaty. The covenant with Noah is a "unilateral promise of God, and it makes no difference what Noah does," since it is made despite full knowledge that "the thoughts of a man's mind are evil from childhood."[8] It is Yahweh who looks at the rainbow and remembers thereby to keep his oath. There is even the implied self-maledictory oath (bow turned toward him) in the rainbow. The Noaic covenant is a "covenant of grant" (Gen. 6:8–9), a unilateral divine oath. "The covenant with Abraham is similar in intent."[9]

> Like the covenant with Noah, that with Abraham binds only God. God obligates himself here to give Abraham Canaan, "the land of the Amorites." What makes this ancient account eerily impressive is the bold way in which it depicts Yahweh as swearing to Abraham. . . . This shares with Sinai only the name "covenant"; the roles of the partners are strikingly different.[10]

One might reply that the command to circumcise certainly represents a condition of inheriting the Abrahamic promise. However, this rite is not treated as a condition of inheritance but as a sign and seal of the inheritance for the heir who is already entitled to it.

> Circumcision is "the *sign* of the covenant between us" ([Gen.] 17:11). It is a mark to identify those who share in the promise God makes and functions like the rainbow to make God remember his own. Of course, anyone lacking this sign does not receive his share, but this is still not a command like those of the Decalogue. The setting and function are quite different. When St. Paul contrasts law and promise and declares: "God gave to Abraham through

a promise," we have to admit that at this point he is right. . . . It would be going too far to say that this sort of covenant represents a religious idea contradictory to the Sinai covenant. As we saw, a pact like that reported in Exodus 20 lays obligations only on the subjects, and yet the Lord, it is assumed, will also behave in a just and righteous way. It is not an instrument for establishing a tyranny. Conversely, even though a covenant like that with Abraham does not spell out how Abraham is to behave, it is assumed in the relation—that of having Yahweh as God—that Abraham will continue to trust God and walk righteously before him. Yet, granting all this, the emphasis in each of the two is so different that they come very close to being opposites.[11]

So far, then, it is possible to distinguish between the straightforward suzerainty treaty of Sinai and the royal grant more indicative of the covenants with Noah and Abraham. We could even include the promise made to Adam after the fall—the so-called *protoeuangelion*, as a type of unconditional royal grant treaty. Unlike the obvious conditionality of the first arrangement with Adam, Genesis 3 promises Adam and Eve a messianic seed who will undo the damage they have caused in their alliance with the serpent. We will explore this more fully in chapter 4.

For our purposes, however, even in Deuteronomy the provisional character of the covenant of law (Sinai) is apparent. Even there, before the people have violated the terms of the treaty, the real hope that transcends national destiny in a typological land is anchored in the Abrahamic promise. Hillers observes:

> The Sinai covenant offered little grounds for optimism, but some hope could be garnered from the promise to Abraham. "When you are in distress and all these things have overtaken you, in the latter time, then you will return to Yahweh your god and hearken to his voice, for Yahweh your god is a merciful god who will not let you down or destroy you, and who will not forget the covenant with your fathers, that which he swore to them" (4:30–31).[12]

Remarkably, the rise of the monarchy is anticipated here (assuming that Deuteronomy was at least in the main compiled during Moses's tenure). In fact, in Deuteronomy 17:14–20 there is a great example of what the Great King to come must fulfill. So even in the Law itself, which emphasizes the personal obligation of each Israelite to fulfill the terms of the national covenant, the attention shifts to the representative king who fulfills Israel's personal obligation and therefore the terms of the everlasting covenant. Thus, it is not only the case that the covenant of promise (Abraham and his seed) appears as the solitary basis for real hope already in the Old Testament, but that it appears already in the Law itself—that is, the Law considered as Torah, the part of the Old Testament that is particularly concerned with the giving of the commands at Mount Sinai. No wonder we read in John's Gospel that "the law was given through Moses; grace and truth came through Jesus Christ" (1:17 NIV) and that Jesus is "the one Moses wrote about in the Law, and about whom the prophets also wrote" (1:45 NIV).

The line from Abraham to his seed runs through David. While the Sinaitic covenant operates on the principle of an approximate national fidelity, the Davidic covenant grows out of the soil of the covenant of promise. You will recall that a covenant of grant (distinguished from a suzerainty treaty) is an outright gift or deed of land and title given in view of past performance, not depending on present or future accomplishments. Although the performance of David's heirs does not figure into this at all (a point emphasized in 1 Sam. 7:1–29; 2 Sam. 23:1–5, and Psalm 89), the Suzerain makes this royal grant in view of David's past faithfulness, which even his own present and future sins cannot annul. In this respect, David is a type of Christ, who receives his inheritance (covenant of grant) on the basis of his past performance—his victory over sin and death, and his brothers and sisters inherit his land, title, and riches simply by their union with him through faith.

The connection between the Abrahamic and Davidic covenants is even more closely established when we return to Genesis 15:1

and read these words spoken to Abraham: "Your reward shall be very great." As Kline points out,

> The term *sakar*, "reward," is used for the compensation due to those who have conducted a military campaign. In Ezekiel 29:19 it refers to the spoil of Egypt which the lord gives Nebuchadnezzar as wages for his army (cf. Isa. 40:10; 62:11). The imagery of Genesis 15:1 is that of the Great King honoring Abraham's notable exhibition of compliance with covenant duty by the reward of a special grant that would more than make up for whatever enrichment he had foregone at the hands of the king of Sodom for the sake of faithfulness to Yahweh, his Lord.[13]

Later in the story, God further rewards Abraham's obedience, when he is willing to offer up his son Isaac (Gen. 22:16–18). It is because of Abraham's faithfulness that Isaac and his heirs will now receive the outcome of the promises (Gen. 26:2ff.). Again, this is not the basis of Abraham's salvation, but the means through which that blessing comes to Abraham's heirs. "God was pleased," writes Kline, "to constitute Abraham's exemplary works as the meritorious ground for granting to Israel after the flesh the distinctive role of being formed as the typological kingdom, the matrix from which Christ should come."[14] This does not mean, of course, that his obedience was the ground of his justification before God (which would contradict Genesis 15:6 and its New Testament interpretation), but that it was itself typological of Christ, who would merit by his obedience the reward of everlasting life that this old covenant economy foreshadowed.

Even in the covenant of redemption, that pact made between the persons of the Godhead in eternity, the elect were given to the Son as a reward for the obedience that he would render on their behalf, in both his life and his death, as well as in his resurrection-victory over the enemies of God and his people. Like the covenants with Noah and Abraham, the covenant with David is anything but conditional and temporary. In 2 Samuel 23:1–5, God promises to establish an "everlasting covenant" with David and his seed, even though he knows they will sin and corrupt his holy hill. Again, this is similar to the covenant with Noah, in which God swears unilaterally not to send a flood even though he knows that the thoughts of human beings are "only evil continually" (Gen. 6:5 KJV).

As we concluded our last chapter, the cleavage between two covenant types had begun to open with the arrival of David as king. The cleavage was already there with Abraham, as we have seen, but now, with the appearance of David,

> the tradition of the covenant with Abraham became the pattern of a covenant between Yahweh and David, whereby Yahweh promised to maintain the Davidic line on the throne (2 Sam. 23:5). Yahweh bound Himself, exactly as in the Abrahamic and Noachite covenant, and therefore Israel could not escape responsibility to the king. The covenant with Abraham was the "prophecy" and that with David the "fulfillment." . . . The Mosaic legal tradition could hardly have been any more attractive to Solomon than it was to Paul.[15]

Only with the eighth-century BC prophets does the Mosaic covenant come back into view, along with the correspondences to the Hittite treaties. At this juncture in Israel's history, then, it is "back to the federation." The rediscovery of the book of the law led to a thorough house cleaning.

> The king [Josiah] together with the people entered into covenant (before the Lord: i.e., with Yahweh as witness, not as a *party* to the covenant) to keep the commandments of the Lord. . . . It brought home to Josiah and the religious leadership that they had been living in a fool's paradise in their assumption that Yahweh had irrevocably committed Himself to preserve the nation in the Davidic-Abrahamic covenant. Moses was rediscovered after having been dormant for nearly three and a half centuries.[16]

These eighth-century Israelites were astonished to realize that the covenant "provided for curses as well as blessings (2 Kings 22:13)."[17]

It is hardly anti-Semitic to observe that the covenant with Israel as a national entity in league with God was conditional and that the nation had so thoroughly violated that covenant that its theocratic status was revoked. Dispensationalism and the so-called two-covenant theory currently popular in mainline theology both treat the land promise as eternal and irrevocable, even to the extent that there can be a difference between Israel and the church in God's plan.[18] Both interpretations, however, fail to recognize that the Hebrew Scriptures themselves qualify this national covenant in strictly conditional terms. This is the witness of the Law and the Prophets as well as Jesus and Paul, not to mention the radical Jewish communities of Second Temple Judaism. In fact, nobody in Jesus's day doubted that Israel was in exile as a direct consequence of their corporate disobedience to the terms of the Sinai pact. Furthermore, the New Testament treats the old covenant (largely identified with the Sinaitic pact) as obsolete, having fulfilled its temporary function of providing the scaffolding for the building of the true and everlasting temple.

The sanctions (threats) of the covenant made with God at Sinai must be taken seriously, and whatever continuity necessarily exists between the covenant of grace running through both testaments—the differences even structurally between, on one hand, the covenants with Adam, Abraham, and David concerning a seed and, on the other, the quite contingent and mutually adopted arrangement that distinguishes the Mosaic economy—must not be swept aside by theological prejudice.

Put yourself in the place of the Israelites living under the terms of Sinai. What conclusions do you draw if you are living in exile in your own land under foreign oppression? Has God failed to keep his promises? Have we failed and has God consequently cut us off forever? Will God renew his patronage as our suzerain if we renew our vows and ratchet up our faithfulness to the Law? These questions can only be answered by going back to the Scriptures, which means, of course, the Old Testament (see, for example, Ps. 89:38–39; Jer. 13:12 ff.).

In those Scriptures we find two distinct covenant traditions: one conditional, the other unconditional. Mendenhall tries his hand at explaining the differences:

> The harmonization of the two covenant traditions meant that great emphasis had to be placed upon the divine forgiveness, and this becomes the foundation of the New Covenant predicted by Jeremiah.... The New Covenant of Christianity obviously continued the tradition of the Abrahamic-Davidic covenant with its emphasis upon the Messiah, Son of David. Paul uses the covenant of Abraham to show the temporary validity of the Mosaic covenant, but in spite of this, the basic structure of New Testament religion is actually, as the early church constantly maintained, the continuation of Mosaic religion.[19]

While Mendenhall travels the well-worn path of higher-critical scholarship in drawing conclusions about the underlying historical motives, he nevertheless rightly recognizes that these two covenant traditions run side by side throughout the Old Testament. The Mosaic (Sinai) covenant is an oath of the people swearing personal performance of the conditions for "living long in the land," while the Abrahamic covenant is a promise by God himself that he will unilaterally bring about the salvation of his people through the seed of Abraham.

The Sinai covenant was something in which each family participated, while the covenant with David (like that with Abraham and Noah) was something they heard about—a pact that had been made in their interest but without their partnership.[20] One aspect of this Davidic covenant is that the king becomes Yahweh's son. We see this in the form of a hymn in Psalm 2 (especially v. 7).

> This covenant is such that even wrongdoing cannot break it. The nation may suffer if the king is wicked, for God will chastise them as a father beats an erring son. But the oath of God will stand, even so! There could not be any clearer evidence of the great gulf that is fixed between this and the intention of the Sinai covenant,

where the stress is on Israel's responsibility. The statement here, shaped no doubt by Israel's experience of what David did to Uriah, of Solomon's apostasies, and so on, attests that God is bound to this promise no matter what. But at the same time, although this contrasts sharply with Sinai, there is a transfer from the older covenant pattern. If the older covenant spoke of blessings for obedience and curses for disobedience on the part of all Israel, this covenant now strikes the motif that Israel's history will henceforth be determined by the character of her king.[21]

In fact, in Psalm 89 God's promise to David and his dynasty is practically treated as a principle of natural law, as fixed as the stars in the heavens. Nothing that David and his heirs do or fail to do can keep God from fulfilling this covenant. "The bond made at Sinai is precarious, fragile as the people's faith; the bond with David is as firm as the sun and moon, as reliable as God."[22]

Catholic Bible scholar Steven L. McKenzie also points to the obvious differences between the Sinaitic and Davidic covenants in terms of their conditional versus promissory character. In Numbers 25:12–13 we have a clear instance of a royal grant given in view of past heroism. Davidic covenant passages include 2 Samuel 7 (cf. 23:5; 1 Kings 8:15–26; 9:1–9; 15:4–5; 1 Chron. 17; 22:12–13; 28:7–10; 2 Chron. 6:4–17; 7:12–22; 21:7; Psalms 89; 132; Isa. 55:3; Jer. 33:14–26). In 2 Samuel 7 the pure divine condescension (promissory covenant) is underscored (especially v. 5, with the emphatic "you"). David wants to build a house for God, but the Davidic covenant is a unilateral promise of God to build a house for David. "It is this promise of an eternal royal line that essentially constitutes the covenant with David."[23] As early as David's son Solomon, the vassal is unworthy and yet the treaty is unaffected (1 Kings 11:29–39). Israel had, for all intents and purposes, so violated the treaty that God's continued presence could remain only "for the sake of his servant David" (2 Kings 8:19; 20:6; cf. 1 Kings 11:34; 15:4–5 NIV)—which means the same thing as "for the sake of Abraham/the fathers" and ultimately in retrospect (i.e., looking back from the New Testament), "for the sake of Christ," the seed of Abraham. Thus, whenever God shows leniency by not executing the curses of the covenant upon Israel's transgression, the basis of such leniency is never the Sinaitic covenant itself, but the Abrahamic (or Davidic) (cf. 2 Kings 13:23). There is no mercy in the Sinaitic covenant itself. It is strictly an oath of allegiance by the people to personally perform everything commanded in the book of the law, with long life in the land promised as the blessing and exile and death as the curse.

Again, behind the covenant at Sinai lie the events of the Abrahamic covenant and its partial fulfillment in the exodus of the Israelites from Egypt under Moses. The relationship between God and Israel is not based entirely on law. After all, God chose Israel and redeemed them from Egypt not because of their own righteousness, but because of his tender mercy (Deuteronomy 6–8). Their being saved from Egyptian captivity and brought into the Promised Land is a matter of grace, pure covenant grant (Gen. 26:5). So also is the status of every Israelite as a justified person in God's sight: all by grace alone, through faith alone, in Christ alone, according to the Abrahamic covenant. However, once in the land, it is up to Israel *as a nation* to determine whether it will remain in God's land or be evicted from it. The unilateral and utterly promissory character of the Abrahamic covenant yields to the conditional arrangement at Sinai even while the former is never—can never be—revoked by the oath-taking God.

Our next chapter will carry forward this two-covenant theology into the Prophets and finally to the inauguration of the new covenant in Jesus Christ.

4

A New Covenant

THE MOST DIFFICULT part of our argument lies behind us. After all, if we can find a covenant of promise and a covenant of law even in the part of the Bible known simply as "the Law," then the differences between these two covenants should become even clearer in the Prophets. That indeed seems to be the case, and the reason is not surprising. As Israel's history unfolds, it becomes clear that Israel was no more successful than Adam in bringing about in God's garden rest from sin, injustice, war, strife, hatred, and oppression. If the principle of personal obligation as the condition for blessing were the basis for judgment, there would be no hope in either case. However, in both Adam's and Israel's cases after their fall, another word is spoken, a word of promise rather than command—an oath taken by God to fulfill his purposes despite human sinfulness.

The "Two Covenants" in the Prophets

Even where the term *covenant* does not appear, it is the backdrop. For instance, the verb *yada'* ("to know") is part of the formal treaty language and belongs prominently to the literary pattern that scholars call the "covenant lawsuit," which is found throughout the Prophets. In fact, the Prophets are more than anything else covenant attorneys, representing the claims of God to the people and vice versa.

Knowing only Yahweh had its corollary in the secular treaties in which the vassal was expected to avoid any entanglements with other suzerains. The implication was for the vassal to legally acknowledge the suzerain as one's superior, not simply to know of the arrangement as an item of information. As Israel acknowledges only Yahweh as their God, Yahweh acknowledges Israel alone as his people. God's word to Israel through Amos was, "You only have I known of all the families of the earth" (3:2 NKJV). (Amos' shift from intimate second-person discourse to the more distant third-person address against the nations is suggestive.[1]) The same idea is found in Jeremiah 24:7 and Hosea 13:4–5. What is obvious is that this "knowing" cannot be reduced either to a mystical or intellectual enterprise. It involves *covenant partnership.*

The "covenant lawsuit" is actually a specific biblical genre.[2] In addition to the obvious courtroom scene, "There is often a call to heaven and earth, or to the mountains and the hills, to serve as witnesses, and there is a summons to the defendant, Israel."[3] Examples of this abound (Deuteronomy 32; Isa. 1:2–3; Jer. 2:4–13; Micah 6:1–8). Just as the covenants were made in history and broken in history, the lawsuits recount the history and base their allegations on historical actions. The threat of sending wild animals to destroy covenant-breakers, found in secular treaties as well as biblical (see Lev. 26:22), has its counterpart in the blessing, "I will remove savage beasts from the land" (26:6 NIV). "No lion will be there, nor will any ferocious beast get up on it [the Way of Holiness]" (Isa. 35:9 NIV). Many of the curses are strikingly similar and in many cases even identical to those of the secular treaties: no descendants, no more singing, a cessation of the sounds of a vibrant city, mothers with empty breasts, a siege of such severity that parents will cannibalize their own children to stay alive, no one to bury the dead, and so on.

Jeremiah 31 famously announces the new covenant in some of its clearest tones. Even though the Israelites have broken the covenant they made at Sinai, Yahweh nevertheless promises a new covenant in which the blessings of the Abrahamic covenant will finally be realized. God's people will be circumcised not only outwardly, but inwardly: they will be given new hearts. The law will not simply be externally imposed upon them, but will be written on their hearts. All of this will happen because God "will forgive their wickedness and will remember their sins no more" (v. 34 NIV).

Thus, the contrast between law and gospel, an external command and an internal willingness, conditions and promises, the letter and the Spirit, does not originate with Paul but with the Old Testament Scriptures, and the book of Jeremiah is among the most obvious in this respect. In fact, God firmly says through Jeremiah that this new covenant "will not be like the covenant I made with their forefathers when I took them by the hand to lead them out of Egypt, *because they broke* my covenant, though I was a husband to them" (31:32 NIV). The point could not be clearer: the new covenant is not a renewal of the old covenant made at Sinai, but an entirely different covenant with an entirely different basis.

With God's words, "They broke my covenant, though I was a husband to them," Jeremiah—who had experienced Josiah's reforms and the hopes of a revival—"dismisses the old order laconically but finally."[4] Whatever its similarities, this new covenant "will come from Yahweh's initiative; it will not be a king's program of reform. And its contents can be summed up in the old formula: 'I will be their God and they will be my people.' . . . This state of affairs will come about because Yahweh will forgive their iniquity and forget their sin."[5]

Under Josiah's reforms, the covenant of Sinai is renewed. As 2 Kings 23 indicates, here the covenant is "before Yahweh," not

"I-you" nor initiated by Yahweh. "It is entirely the idea of the king and the people."[6] It is the *people's* promise, not the *Lord's*. This is the pattern we find in the postexilic renewals (2 Kings 11:17; 2 Chron. 23:3; Ezra 9–10; Nehemiah 9–10). King Josiah and all the people renew the covenant "in the presence of the LORD" (2 Kings 23:3 NIV). Such a renewal of the Sinaitic covenant takes place with the rediscovery of the book of the law, and then the returning exiles join in this renewal (Ezra 10:3). This would become the pattern for the successive renewal movements all the way to Jesus's day: by rededicating themselves to the oath they took at Sinai, the nation would throw off the oppressor and prepare the land for the reign of Messiah. This is why the Pharisees were so scrupulous in their attention to the minutiae of Old Testament legislation.

If it is wrong to say that the Sinai covenant is simply *identical* to the Abrahamic covenant of grace, it is not quite right to say that the Sinai covenant (hence, the theocracy generally) is *nothing more than* a republication of the original covenant of works made to Adam before the fall. Before the fall, there was no need for grace. God did all things well, and at the pinnacle of creation stood the holy image-bearer who reflected the glory of God in every way possible for a creature. In this I agree with the old Reformed theologians, M. G. Kline, and many others.

At the same time, it is also true that after the fall *all* covenants were founded on historical prologues that were indisputably gracious in character. As we have seen, Israel was not chosen and liberated from Egypt because of their righteousness. Even the Decalogue begins with the exodus liberation event. This is a straightforward suzerainty treaty: "I have done X. Therefore, you do Y." At the same time, what happens at Sinai itself is not gracious. This pact made by the people establishes personal obedience to every commandment as the basis for life in the land. The nation-state can break God's covenant; the land promises are temporary and conditional, as Adam's probation was. They are not the final, ultimate reality.

As the Israelites show repeatedly, even early on in the pilgrimage from Egypt, a simple pledge, "We will do all of this," will not do. There must be provision for transgression; hence, the sacrifices. The "blood of the covenant" is an early theme in the Pentateuch, not only with the ritual putting the covenant into effect, but in the symbolic nature of the blood being poured out on the mercy seat in the tabernacle between the horns of the ark of the covenant itself and covering the broken tablets inside the ark. Thus, we can conclude that although the Sinai covenant is gracious in terms of the history leading up to it and in the fact that through Moses's intercession and the sacrifices provision is made for temporarily appeasing God's anger, ultimately Israel's tenure in the land—given to Israel by divine grace—is lost by disobedience.

The missing piece here is "for the sake of your fathers." As we have seen, every event of divine restraint throughout Israel's history of rebellion is explained by Yahweh himself in terms of his commitment (*hesed*) to the Abrahamic covenant, not the Sinaitic covenant. It is God's *immutable* covenant that provides for a certain latitude or patience on God's part, although according to the terms of Sinai, Israel could have been judged finally much sooner and eventually was judged. Once Messiah does appear, the old covenant (Sinai) is no longer necessary, as the reality displaces its types and shadows. So the Messiah announces, in the Spirit of the prophets, the "curses" upon national Israel. So Paul announces, in the Spirit of Christ, the absolute antithesis of Sinai and Zion, Hagar (ironically and even scandalously paralleled with the earthly Jerusalem—in union with Moses) and Sarah (identified with the heavenly Jerusalem—in union with Abraham and Christ). The Israelites of Jesus's and Paul's day had misidentified themselves with Abraham, Sarah, and Zion when in fact they were simply under a covenant of law. They thought they were justified according to the terms of Sinai when in fact they were only condemned by it. The only hope, for Jew and Gentile, is to be incorporated into Abraham—the "heavenly Jerusalem"—by union with Christ through faith alone.

The promissory covenant is realized through David just as it is through the patriarchs—not through their own personal obedience as somehow mediating redemption, but through their seed (in David's case, the Son of David whose throne will be "everlasting") and the personal obedience of this Son of David who is greater than Solomon. It is not through his own personal kingship that David would bring salvation (i.e., through the monarchy instead of federative family covenants), but through the "everlasting throne"—the everlasting dynasty that would be established by the Son of David, Messiah. Only through Sinai could Israel be established in the land—by the personal loyalty of the people themselves to the covenant. But only through the covenant of *promise* could anyone—Israelite or Gentile—become children of Abraham in the sense identified in the New Testament. Like the Abrahamic covenant, the Davidic covenant is unilateral and unconditional. And only in that way could the blessings flow to the ends of the earth and not just to the Jews, just as the Abrahamic promise intended.

Yahweh established David in the same way he sovereignly made Abraham his beneficiary. This is royal grant language, not suzerainty treaty language. While many interpreters simply collapse these two types of covenants into one, others (such as Hillers) go too far in the other direction, concluding that the whole notion of covenant is conditional and that the New Testament therefore gives it up entirely in favor of *diatheke*, which usually referred to a "last will and testament." Both answers fail to explain the biblical data.

The New Testament does not end up without a doctrine of covenant, but it does end up with a *royal grant* that is absolutely consistent with a "last will and testament." This royal grant is one-sided in terms of its basis yet calls for genuine partnership and future obedience as the reasonable response. Further, if we are to read about the kingship canonically, we find that this royal grant is made (as usually in the ancient world) on the basis of David's own past performance. Yet does this square with Paul's appeal in

Romans 4 to David as an example of one who, like Abraham, is justified by faith alone apart from works?

A contradiction only emerges if we fail to distinguish between the typological and conditional aspects of the old covenant (based on the law) and the reality to which they point (based on promise). Like Abraham, David is the recipient of a covenant of grant because of past performance, but this royal grant concerns the perpetuity of his seed on the throne (as it did Abraham's in the land), not individual salvation.

Only the greater Son of Abraham and David is able to merit by his covenant faithfulness the everlasting blessings that the earthly Canaan and throne of David merely anticipate typologically. Therefore, together with us, Abraham and David inherit by grace through faith alone, on the basis of Christ's meritorious exploits alone, the true City of God, seated with Christ in heavenly places.

Even more clearly than Abraham's, David's military campaigns presage the greater victory of his greater Son, receiving a greater prize for his conquest. With respect to individual salvation, therefore, Abraham, David, and the rest of us receive the eternal inheritance not by personal performance (past, present, and future), but on the basis of Christ's performance. This bounty is then inherited by us as a last will and testament.

Abraham and David have nothing to say about the matter. Their personal mistakes (amply recorded) are incapable of thwarting God's purposes. They must simply believe the promise.

Second Temple Judaism

Referring to the period between the Old and New Testaments when Herod's temple replaced Solomon's original structure, Second Temple Judaism is the context in which a rich variety of end-times expectations swirled about. It was the era in which a virgin was told that she would conceive and bring forth a savior.

It is impossible to treat the whole spectrum of Jewish belief in the Second Temple period. However, we will briefly analyze the Essene covenant theology as a bridge to our discussion of the concept's development in the New Testament.

Contemporaries of the Pharisees and Sadducees, the Essenes, centered at Qumran, were destroyed in the uprising against Rome in 68 AD. The first discoveries in the caves were made in 1947. Qumran used *covenant* (*berit*) "over five times as often as do the New Testament writers" and even used the term *new covenant*.[7] The *Manual of Discipline* is the Qumran community's constitution, and although it begins with the requirement that the congregation be chided for their sins and plead divine forgiveness, entering into a covenant appears quite clearly a matter of personal obedience.

> He shall swear, by a binding oath, that as he lives he will return to the Law of Moses according to all he commanded, with all his heart and soul. . . . When anyone enters into the covenant to do according to all these precepts, and to be united to the holy assembly, they shall jointly and in common investigate his spirit, with respect to his intelligence and his obedience to the Law . . . according to his intelligence and his deeds.[8]

The *Damascus Document*, part of the Essene corpus, sees the world in stark terms of light and darkness, the righteous and the wicked, those who perfectly conform in heart and life to the law and the covenant-breakers. Eternal life will be given to those who fulfill God's righteous commands, while eternal destruction awaits all who transgress. Those who in any way associate with Gentiles or uncleanness disqualify themselves from an inheritance at the end of the age. While the Pharisees were willing to remain in Jerusalem, attempting to purge the people of wickedness and dedi- cate themselves to Torah and temple, the Essenes had given up on the possibility of reform in Jerusalem. They would be God's faithful remnant out in the desert, preparing for Messiah by pure worship, while the Jerusalem elite would be swept along with the Gentiles in the stream of God's judgment. The "new covenant" for them is clearly a covenant of law. Unlike Jeremiah's "new covenant," which is not like the covenant at Sinai, the Essenes saw the new covenant precisely as the repristination or renewal of that legal oath of the people. The new covenant is in truth a renewal of the old.

The New Testament

In a rare instance of an explicit reference to "covenant," our Lord called his own sacrifice—and, as its sign and seal, the supper in the upper room—"my blood of the new testament, which is shed for many for the remission of sins" (Matt. 26:28 KJV). The New Testament maintains a consistent witness to the belief that the identity of belonging to God—in other words, the inheritance—was centered around Christ rather than Sinai. This is why the "new covenant" inaugurated by Christ's sacrifice looks back through Jeremiah 31 to David and Abraham. In Hebrews we read that it is not like the old covenant in that it coalesces around a Son rather than a servant in God's house, a better covenant, one enacted on better promises (see Hebrews 8). The writer says of Jeremiah's prophecy, "By calling this covenant 'new,' he has made the first one obsolete; and what is obsolete and aging will soon disappear" (8:13 NIV; see also 9:11–23). All attention shifts from Israel, the oath-taking party at Sinai, to Christ, the seed of Abraham and Son of David. The sacrificial system of the old covenant never did take away sins but only reminded worshipers of their transgressions, while the sacrifice of Christ is perfect and takes away sin forever, ushering all worshipers into the Holy of Holies behind the veil that separated the glory of God from the people.

In Hebrews 10:28–29, the writer sharply contrasts this older covenantal understanding (Sinai) with the new. Just as the blessings of being in Christ are greater than being in Moses, the curses are greater for those who still place their faith in the shadows of the law rather than in the promises of the gospel. Like Paul, then, the writer to the Hebrews contrasts the typological covenant of law (Sinai) with the covenant of promise (Abrahamic). While the old covenant has passed away, the Abrahamic covenant has not.

> For when God made a promise to Abraham, because He could swear by no one greater, He swore by Himself, saying, "Surely blessing I will bless you, and multiplying I will multiply you." And so, after he had patiently endured, he obtained the promise. For men indeed swear by the greater, and an oath for confirmation is for them an end of all dispute. Thus God, determining to show more abundantly to the heirs of promise the immutability of His counsel, confirmed it by an oath, that by two immutable things, in which it is impossible for God to lie, we might have strong consolation, who have fled for refuge to lay hold of the hope set before us.
>
> Hebrews 6:13–18 NKJV

So just as in Galatians, the point is pressed that those who seek to obtain the blessing and avoid the curse by their personal obedience (i.e., the Sinai covenant) are already condemned, while those who seek that blessing by inheritance in Christ alone (i.e., the Abrahamic covenant) are the true heirs according to promise.

In Paul's epistles we also see the old and new covenants elaborated in terms of a movement from the lesser to the greater. In this sense, law (identified with the old covenant) and gospel (identified with the new covenant) are complementary: the sacrifices and the temple point forward to Christ. But Paul is not only thinking of the progress from the old to the new covenant. He also has in mind the difference between the Abrahamic covenant of promise and the Sinaitic covenant of law. When it comes to how we receive the inheritance and so are made beneficiaries of everlasting life, Paul sets these covenants in absolute antithesis. They represent two different "principles" (*nomoi*): the principle of works (law) and the principle of grace (promise).

If we identify the old covenant primarily with the Sinaitic covenant of law, we end up with contrasts such as these in 2 Corinthians 3:

an old covenant written on tables of stone versus a new covenant written on human hearts; a written code versus God's own Spirit; death-dealing versus life-giving; a dispensation of death versus a dispensation of the Spirit; condemnation versus righteousness; fading versus permanent; veiled versus unveiled glory.

At the same time, it is important to recognize that it was not Paul who introduced a law-promise, Sinai-Abraham, Moses-Christ contrast. Jesus himself did this, especially in pronouncing the covenant curses ("woes"), condemning the "right" of the religious leaders, and in redrawing the true Israel around himself rather than Temple and Torah. The parables underscore this point, especially the story of the publican and the Pharisee (Luke 18:9–14), the cursing of the fig tree followed by his judgment on the temple (Mark 11:12–25), the parable of the wicked tenants (Mark 12:1–12) and the two sons (Matt. 21:28–32). There are also his statements about the true children of Abraham (John 8:39, 59), not to mention his interaction with the rich young ruler in Mark 10:17–31. Reference could also be made to Jesus's teaching in Luke 16:14–17. Peter's viewpoint was transformed when the clean-unclean distinction was dramatically dissolved for him in a vision (Acts 10:9–16; 11:1–18). And it was through Jeremiah that God said the new covenant would not be "according to the covenant that I made with their fathers in the day that I took them by the hand to bring them out of the land of Egypt" (Jer. 31:31–32 NKJV).

One of the truly remarkable things about this understanding of Christ's person and work in the light of covenant is that the covenant *Lord* is also the covenant *Servant*. The Son is God, the same God who spoke the creation into existence. In fact, Jesus Christ is the Word by whom all things were made (John 1:3). He is also the divine speaker to humanity in the giving of the command in the Garden of Eden and then again at Mount Sinai. His were the words that shook the mountain and filled the hearers with dread. Yet this same God who spoke the command assumed human flesh and came down the mountain to take the place of the hearers below. While Adam and Eve, as well as Israel, answered back, "All this we will do," yet failed miserably, Jesus became not only the faithful speaker, but the faithful hearer and doer of the Word of God. He not only commanded as the Lord of the covenant, but answered back faithfully as the Servant of the covenant—in our place. No wonder Christ is *everything* in this new covenant relationship!

Covenant vs. Testament?

One of the easiest ways of explaining the difference between conditional (suzerainty) and promissory (grant) covenants has been to treat the Old and New Testaments in terms of the former and latter, respectively. If the New Testament writers wanted to retain the idea of "covenant," they would have used the Greek word *syntheke* rather than *diatheke*, since the former refers to a bilateral agreement. The New Testament writers jettisoned the Old Testament *berit* (covenant) altogether: *diatheke* is not actually a translation of *berit*, but an entirely different concept. A bilateral contract is made between two living parties, while a last will and testament is simply granted to the heirs upon the benefactor's death. Delbert Hillers takes just this view, investigating the relationship between the Last Supper and "new covenant."

> In Moses' use of the words "blood of the covenant," the blood helps bring the curse into effect; the people are identified with the victim, whose fate will be theirs if they sin. The eucharistic words do indeed identify Jesus with his disciples—note that all the versions, at one point or another, have "for you," "on your behalf," or the like—but the emphasis is not on bringing them under a curse but rather of a sacrifice made on their behalf. Thus, though there is a verbal echo of the Sinai covenant, the real conceptual link is to the new covenant of forgiveness of which Jeremiah spoke.[9]

A curse regarding unworthily eating the bread and drinking the cup can be found in 1 Corinthians 11:27. But Hillers concludes that the New Testament does not really have a covenant at all.

Christ's advent has so transformed the notion that it is a shadow of its former self, which it justifies according to the shadow-reality, promise-fulfillment pattern.[10]

Although identifying the covenant concept with a conditional arrangement of law in contrast to promise (last will and testament) would simplify things, doing so just would not fit the evidence. Thus, it is often suggested, although *berit* could have been translated with the Greek equivalent of a bilateral covenant (*syntheke*), the whole notion of covenant is left to the shadows of Sinai and the new covenant is really not a covenant at all, but a *diatheke* (testament), as in a last will and testament.

First, we should note that the seventy scribes who translated the Hebrew Scriptures into Greek (the translation being identified as the Septuagint or simply LXX for "seventy") already translated *berit* as *diatheke* before the appearance of Christ, and it is unlikely that they felt any great burden to surrender the idea of a bilateral covenant to a foreign concept associated not with international treaties but with the disposition of property upon one's death. In that case, it would not be surprising that the New Testament writers would have felt no obligation to select for theological reasons an alternative to *syntheke* simply because they wanted to distance themselves from the Hebraic *berit*. As Steven McKenzie points out, *diatheke* is used thirty-three times in the New Testament (Gospels and Acts: Matt. 26:28; Mark 14:24; Luke 1:72; 22:20; Acts 3:25; 7:8; Paul: Rom. 9:4; 11:27; 1 Cor. 11:25; 2 Cor. 3:6, 14; Gal. 3:15, 17; 4:24; Eph. 2:12; Heb. 7:22; 8:6, 8, 9 [twice], 10; 9:4 [twice], 15 [twice], 16, 17, 20; 10:16, 29; 12:24; 13:20; "ark of the covenant" is mentioned in Rev. 11:19). "This illustrates the dependence of the New Testament on the Hebrew Bible for its perspective on 'covenant' but does not contribute to that perspective per se."[11]

Second, it is important to identify covenants not in terms of the mere appearance of the word (*berit/diatheke*), but in terms of the action taking place and the context in which it is administered. Second Samuel 23:5 is the only reference to the Davidic "covenant" in the entire narrative, and yet the Psalter is pregnant with references (89:3, 19–37, 39; 132:12; cf. Jer. 33:21; Hos. 6:7; 8:1). Hebrews explicitly identifies the promise of an everlasting dynasty to David as a "covenant" and applies it to Christ (Heb. 5:5–6), and Geerhardus Vos has convincingly argued that David himself understood a messianic reference.[12] If it is argued that "covenant" has no standing in the New Testament, it can be equally asserted that "testament" has no standing in the Old.[13]

A third contention is that the prophets themselves identify the fulfillment of God's ancient promises as a "new covenant" (Isa. 59:21; Jer. 31:31–33; 32:40; 50:5; Ezek. 16:60, 62; 20:37; 34:25; 37:26; Hos. 2:18), and that is the understanding of the New Testament writers (1 Cor. 11:25; 2 Cor. 3:6; Gal. 4:24; Heb. 7:22; 9:15).

J. Barton Payne has argued that the entire New Testament doctrine is testament over covenant.[14] Yet O. Palmer Robertson rightly notes that a substitutionary death is necessarily covenantal rather than simply testamentary.

> The provisions of the "last will and testament" inherently presume death to be inevitable, and all its stipulations build on that fact. But the provisions of a covenant offer the options of life or death. . . . Only in the event of covenant violation does actual death of the covenant-maker occur. It is in the context of covenantal death, not testamentary death, that the death of Jesus Christ is to be understood. . . . Yet death in substitution for another has no place whatsoever in the making of a last will and testament. The testator dies in his own place, not in the place of another.[15]

The ordinary use is not what should determine this matter, but the specific use to which the biblical writers put the words. The relationship of *berit* to *diatheke* is not obvious at first.

> Yet death is as inseparably related to "covenant" as to "testament." If the present study of God's covenant with Abraham establishes anything, it indicates the vital relation of death to covenant. Essential to the inauguration both of the Abrahamic and Mosaic covenants was the symbolic representation of the death of the covenant-

maker. The long history of God's terminal judgments on Israel finds prophetic interpretation in the light of God's execution of the death-curse on covenant breakers. Death and covenant clearly relate. They relate concretely in two ways. First, the death of the covenant-maker receives symbolic representation at the time of the inauguration of the covenant. The covenant-making procedure is not complete without this pledge-to-death aspect. Secondly, the death of the covenant-violator receives historical actualization when covenantal judgment is executed. Once a transgression of covenantal commitment has occurred, death is inevitable. So both "testament" and "covenant" involve death. Death activates a testament. Death inaugurates and vindicates a covenant. Clearly the opening verse in this section of Hebrews [9:15–20] is concerned with the relation of death to "covenant."[16]

"The *diatheke* in Hebrews 9:15," Robertson points out, "is the Mosaic covenant. God did not establish through Moses a 'last will and testament.' He established instead a 'covenant.'"[17] This is even more emphatic in verses 17–20. "A testament (singular) is not made firm 'over dead bodies' (plural)."[18] Robertson rejects M. G. Kline's attempt to see a play here between *testament* and *covenant* in terms of dynastic succession provisions.[19] But Robertson (rightly, I think) points out that Hebrews 9 is concerned not with the question of treaty *succession* but treaty *inauguration*.[20] "Making firm" here is *bebaia*; "making strong" is *ischuei*. (In Matthew 26:28 the "pouring out" (*ekcheo*) is clearly sacrificial language and it is "for the remission of sins," not for inheriting a bequest.)

It is not that Abraham has no obligations in the covenant relation. Already he has been required to leave his fatherland (Gen. 12:1ff). Later he shall be required unequivocally to administer the seal of circumcision to all his male descendants (Gen. 17:1, 4). But as the covenant is instituted formally in Genesis 15, the Lord dramatizes the gracious character of the covenantal relation by having himself alone to pass between the pieces. The covenant shall be fulfilled because God assumes to himself full responsibility in seeing to its realization.[21]

This solemn cutting ceremony in Genesis 15, unilateral in character, answers Abraham's question, "How will I know?" It is exactly this same passing through the pieces that Jesus enacts in the Lord's Supper: "Now he offers himself to you. He says: 'Take, eat; this is my body. This is my blood of the covenant shed for many. Drink, all of you, of it.'"[22]

This view not only does greater lexicographical justice; theologically it expands both *berit* and *diatheke* to include the wider range of meanings that are actually apparent in the distinct arrangements that we find across the testaments and links the Lord's Supper to the reality of the host's sacrificial death. Vos argues:

> It is true our Lord establishes a connection between His death and the new *diatheke* inaugurated. But this by no means shuts us up to viewing the *diatheke* as a testament put into effect through the death. The true interpretation of the Lord's Supper is that it appears as a sacrificial meal, to which His death forms the sacrifice. If, therefore, the new *diatheke* is connected with the death of Jesus, the connection will have to be sought along the lines of sacrifice, that is to say, the death must be assumed to give birth to the *diatheke* in the same capacity and for the same reason which make it the central feature of the sacrament. It is, therefore, a priori, probable that the *diatheke* appears as something inaugurated by a sacrifice, and that it is not a "testament" but either a "religious disposition" or a "covenant." The obvious parallel in which Jesus places the blood of the new *diatheke* with that of Exodus 24, where the blood is none other than the blood of sacrifice inaugurating the Sinaitic *berith*, also requires this interpretation. And when it is said of the blood as exponential of the death that it is *huper pollon*, "on behalf of many," this yields a thought utterly incongruous of testament, for a testator does not die in behalf of or with the intent of benefiting his heirs, whereas the benevolent intent of the death of a person fits admirably into the circle of sacrificial ideas.[23]

If we sharply distinguish the Old and New Testaments in terms of *covenant* and *testament*, we reduce the significance of the promise-fulfillment pattern to a minimum. As McKenzie observes, "The image of ratifying a covenant through blood in these passages [institution of the Lord's Supper] and elsewhere in the New Testament (Heb. 10:29; 12:24; 13:20) is borrowed from the covenant-making ceremony in the Hebrew Bible (Exod. 24:8)."[24] We must see the inauguration of the supper in terms of fulfillment (of the *berit*) rather than as a completely new idea in redemptive history. In light especially of Hebrews 9:20 we can see that the reference to "covenant" (*diatheke*) in Jesus's words of institution do not have a last will and testament as their backdrop but rather the sprinkling of blood in Exodus 24 that enacts or inaugurates a covenant.

The problem with the identification of *berit* with synergism (human cooperation in justification and regeneration) is that it represents the imposition of systematic-theological categories that do not allow the word its full range of meaning. Vos notes that the same is true of *diatheke*. Just as *berit* has a broad range of possible meanings, so too does *diatheke*. Derived from the verb generally meaning "to dispose of one's estate/affairs," *diatheke* came to be used in Greek law to refer both to one's last will and testament and, in admittedly less common instances, "treaty" or "mutually obligating law."[25] So the verb could mean "to arrange one's affairs" or, more commonly, "to make a will."[26]

As used in the New Testament, asks Vos, "how could such a thought [prospective death] have been applied to God, who is throughout the maker of the religious *diatheke*? In the New Testament the *diatheke* as a 'last will' is once brought into connection with the sacrifice of Christ, once with the promise of God to Abraham."[27] Finally, in Ephesians 2:12, Paul speaks of "the covenants of the promise," which could hardly be done if covenants are always and only conditional arrangements of reciprocal obligation.

To summarize, we should avoid two errors that lead ultimately to the same confusion. On one hand, we must resist concluding that the covenant concept is inherently conditioned upon personal performance and, on the other, that it is inherently gracious in character. In both cases, we are making a priori judgments about what a covenant can and cannot be rather than attending to the diverse ways in which the word is used in the Scriptures. *Covenant* in both Old and New Testaments, so we have argued, is a broad term encompassing a variety of arrangements—most notably, conditional covenants of law and unconditional covenants of promise. Already in the Old Testament itself there are these two covenant types: suzerainty and royal grant, the latter fitting perfectly the New Testament concept of *diatheke* or "last will and testament." Just as a great king bestows a gift on a loyal vassal in view of noteworthy service, the New Testament teaches that believers become coheirs with Christ, the Servant of Yahweh, inheriting by grace that which he has inherited by personal obedience. His death inaugurates our receipt of that inheritance just as the death of a testator puts the will into effect and disposes of the estate. So the New Testament does not jettison the Old Testament concept of covenant, but rather identifies its new covenant with the royal grant, a promissory oath made to Noah, Abraham, and David.

That Paul offers the contrasts we have indicated above is widely recognized. Some interpreters attempt to make Paul inoffensive to early Jewish belief (emphasizing a single covenant of grace with strong continuity across the two testaments), while others underscore discontinuity to the point of an almost Marcionite identification of the Old Testament exclusively with a now obsolete law, viewing law as an inherently negative category. Others simply find Paul hopelessly contradictory and his arguments difficult if not impossible to vindicate even on his own assumptions.

Paul is only as clear as we allow him to be as he makes fine distinctions that are not original to him but are in fact deeply embedded in the Prophets. For the apostle to the Gentiles, the simplistic identification of the Old Testament with "law" and the New Testament with "grace" is unthinkable. God's covenant of grace, announced beforehand to Adam and inaugurated with Abraham, is precisely the same as to its content in both testaments. Believers in Christ are not a *tertium quid* between Israel and the nations; they are the true children of Abraham, whether Jew or Gentile. Nevertheless, within the Old Testament itself, Paul finds two discrete covenantal traditions: Abrahamic and Sinaitic. Jesus Christ is the fulfillment of the unilateral promises of the first and the typological fulfillment of the bilateral conditions of the second. Thus, he is the true seed of Abraham and also the true Israel, the one who has fulfilled the terms of the covenant at Sinai in the place of those who have *said* "We will do all these things," and yet have in fact fallen short. To belong to God's gracious covenant, one must come by way of Christ rather than Moses—or, as the writer to the Hebrews puts it, Mount Zion rather than Mount Sinai (Heb. 12:22). In Galatians 4, as Geerhardus Vos observes,

> Paul speaks of two contrasting *diathekai*, i.e., two great religious systems operating by diverse methods and with opposite results, the one a Hagar-*diatheke*, geographically associated with Mount Sinai, the other a Sarah-*diatheke*, having its local center in the heavenly Jerusalem. There is a difference between this and II Corinthians 3 insofar as there the old and the new were contrasted in their original God-willed and God-given character, whilst here in Galatians the Sinaitic-Hagar *diatheke* is *the old system as perverted by Judaism*. But the comparative manner of handling the idea is the same in both passages and in both cases is alike responsible for its introduction.[28]

Despite his willingness to contrast old and new orders, the apostle uses *diatheke* as the common term: not "old law"/"new law," but "old covenant"/"new covenant," "since in its fundamental aspects it transcends the category of law, and since precisely in this supra-legal character consists a large part of the superiority of the Christian state which the author is intent upon bringing out."[29]

That those who trusted in the promise made to Abraham were saved throughout the old covenant history Paul does not doubt (in fact, he interprets the OT christologically, as in 1 Cor. 10:4, 9). Yet the Sinaitic covenant (i.e., the theocracy) was a parenthesis in God's redemptive plot, a means of bringing life to the whole world through Abraham's seed, just as the patriarch was promised in Genesis 15: "a father of many nations."

Paul's opponents also claimed Jeremiah 31 and the promise of a new covenant being fulfilled in their midst. As we have seen, the Essene sect also claimed to belong to the new covenant, but as a renewal of the old. It would hardly be stretching to suggest that Paul's opponents in this Galatian debate claim to be ministers of the new covenant but, despite their acceptance of Christ, also view that new covenant as a renewal of the old. That would explain why the apostle goes back behind Sinai and Moses to Abraham as the basis for the new covenant. When the question of how we, Jews and Gentiles together, inherit the blessing that God promised, the covenants of law and promise are set in absolute opposition. Paul is insisting that his opponents have, like their non-Christian Jewish contemporaries, failed to recognize in their own Hebrew Scriptures the contrast between these two covenants.

The new covenant, as prophesied by Jeremiah and exhibited in the New Testament, is not wholly inimical to Moses qua Moses or Israel qua Israel. Indeed, Moses entreated the people on the plains of Moab to circumcise the foreskins of the heart (Deut. 10:16; 30:6). The problem was that they could not do this, although they promised to do so. It is not in the *goal* that the Sinaitic differs from the Abrahamic covenant, but in the *potency*. Commands issue from Sinai with smoke and peals of thunder, but there is nothing distinctive in the Mosaic economy that actually provides for its fulfillment. True, there are provisions for forgiveness in the sacrifices: though these are mere shadows and cannot themselves take away sin, they are true means of grace, genuine means of clinging to God's forgiveness that will be secured by the sacrifice of Christ. But there is no specific provision for each Israelite to be circumcised in heart. The command is just and good, but the ability to perform it is not present (Romans 7). By contrast, in Jesus's Sermon on the Mount he pronounces blessing on those who cannot circumcise their own hearts (Matt. 5:1–11). In fact, Jesus does not cancel the law but rather upholds it: the basis for acceptance remains perfect righteousness (v. 20). The question is whether that righteousness is inherent in us or imputed to us—and one thing that Jesus's subsequent interpretation of the law makes clear is that if it is the former, we are utterly without hope (vv. 21–48).

It is only in the new covenant as the realization of the Abrahamic-Davidic covenant that this release from sin's bondage and guilt is actually secured. "But what the law was powerless to do, God did by sending his Son. . . ." So expressly is the old covenant identified (in the sharpest contrast) at this point with Moses that Paul could say, "If you let yourselves be circumcised, Christ will be of no benefit to you" (Gal. 5:2 NRSV).

It is clear from many other places in Paul that he could not have meant that circumcision did not benefit the saints under the old covenant, much less that baptism does not now benefit saints under the new. Rather, he is warning his opponents whose trust in circumcision is but the tip of the iceberg of their trust in the shadows of the law that—in the meaning they attach to it—they have cut themselves off from the promise that circumcision itself was inaugurated to represent and seal.

It is difficult to imagine a more ironic distortion of circumcision's original intent than that employed by the Galatian heretics. That circumcision is but representative of the reliance on works more generally is not only attested in Galatians but in Romans 4, where "works of the law" and simply "works" are juxtaposed to "faith" and "promise." Abraham was not only justified before he was circumcised; he was justified *apart from* works *while he was still ungodly* in himself. The point is not simply that God justifies the *uncircumcised*, but that God justifies *the wicked*. If justification had only been a matter of circumcision or noncircumcision, Paul never would have insulted his readers by implying that they did not understand that right standing before God comes through faith and not works (Romans 10). It is whether God justifies the wicked qua wicked, on the basis of another's righteousness, that is contested by some in Paul's audience.

So then we can affirm concerning the Abrahamic covenant that it was not a bilateral or suzerainty covenant at all.

> It was a disposition-*berith* in the strictest sense, intended exclusively by God for the purpose of binding Himself in the strongest possible way by His own promise, and so rendering the promise unalterably sure. It is for nothing else than for faithfully translating this import of the *berith* into the thought-form of his readers and so bringing it home to their understanding that Paul says God made with Abraham a testamental *diatheke*.[30]

As we learn from Stephen's martyrdom sermon in Acts, "First God gave a promise-*berith*, then He imposed a law-*berith*. So Genesis intends it and so Stephen quotes it."[31] This is also Paul's understanding in Galatians, where he argues that the former, Abrahamic promise cannot be set aside by the later law *berit*. Robertson is right when he says:

> Israel's national devastation may be understood only in terms of the Mosaic covenant. The Davidic covenant indeed was in effect. But it was Israel's violation of the stipulations of the Mosaic covenant that finally determined the inevitability of their captivity. Because Israel would not keep God's commandments and statutes according to the law of Moses, exile occurred (cf. 2 Kings 17:13ff).[32]

Yet, in the very next sentence he concludes from this fact, "The history of God's covenant people indicates that the covenants basically are one. The Abrahamic, Mosaic, and Davidic covenants do not supplant one another; they supplement one another. A basic unity binds them together." However, the logic of his own argument would seem to suggest greater distinction between the conditional and unconditional covenants in Israel's history.

The promissory oath (Abrahamic covenant) "underlies the whole subsequent development; it is the broad basis on which the two successive covenants rest."[33] The Sinai covenant is the one realized in a temporal typological kingdom; the Abrahamic is

realized in the heavenly eschatological kingdom. Through revelation (God to humanity) and priesthood (humanity to God), God
himself secures the covenant movement back and forth between
God and humanity.[34] "His is the originality in conceiving, His the
initiative in inaugurating, His the monergism in carrying out."[35]
"For of Him and through Him and to Him are all things, to
whom be glory forever. Amen" (Rom. 11:36 NKJV). Only the new
covenant can create true worshipers. "Legalism lacks the supreme
sense of worship. It obeys but it does not adore."[36]

Conclusions

Few have done more to highlight the covenantal architecture of
Scripture than Old Testament scholar Walther Eichrodt. However,
he failed, as much of biblical and theological scholarship has, to
recognize the diverse ways in which *covenant* can be put to use
in the Scriptures. Roman Catholic scholar Dennis J. McCarthy
criticizes Eichrodt and others on just this point: "The historical relationships, and ideological differences, of the Abrahamic,
Mosaic and Davidic covenants are glossed over in the necessity to
subordinate the entire Old Testament material to the one covenant
of Mount Sinai."[37] McCarthy also argues (as does Hillers) that
there is a noticeable transfer of emphasis from the Sinai covenant
to the Abrahamic covenant in which hopes are renewed, especially
in the Prophets. "Thus the promissory covenant, whether Davidic
or patriarchal, has an important theological role."[38] On the basis
of comparing it to the secular treaties, McCarthy judges that the
Davidic covenant cannot be reduced to a suzerain-vassal treaty
with mutual obligations and curses.[39] "Further, the permanence
of the Davidic covenant as described in the basic statement of it is
not dependent upon the fidelity of the Davidics; on the contrary,
the promise of Nathan says explicitly that even though the king is
faithless, his position will be assured. This is the direct contrary
of the case in the formal treaty."[40]

In preparing for the next chapter, then, I hope to have made the following biblical-theological arguments:

A. Concerning the covenantal unity of the two testaments:
  1. "Law" and "promise" do not represent the Old and New Testaments or *berit* and *diatheke*, respectively, but characterize two different kinds of covenants that obtain within the same history.
  2. No less than new covenant believers, those under the old covenant were united to Christ by faith in the promise that was heard, although it could only be adumbrated under the figures of the Mosaic economy.
B. Concerning the covenantal discontinuity within the two testaments:
  1. The covenants with Adam after the fall, as with Noah, Abraham, and David, represent unconditional divine oaths. In these instances, Yahweh (the suzerain) freely and mercifully obligates himself to fulfill a promise despite the opposition he encounters even from the beneficiaries of the oath. We may call these "royal grants," "promissory oaths," "unconditional dispositions," or any number of terms drawn from ancient legal custom, but they are distinguished sharply from suzerainty pacts in which a greater party (suzerain) obligates a lesser party (vassal) to serve faithfully and in which blessings or curses are held out as recompense.
  2. This latter type of covenant is constitutive for the pact between Yahweh and Israel at Sinai through its successive cycles of violation, restoration, transgression, and finally exile. Although this covenant governing the theocracy served a vital pedagogical function, making Israel aware of their sinfulness and need for atonement, even anticipating that atonement through the elaborate sacrificial and temple system, it could not take away sin and left all who sought to be justified by it under its curse. So while it is true

that Old Testament saints were justified by faith according
to the Abrahamic promise, the theocracy itself was to be
maintained and vindicated by strict adherence to Torah.
3. In this light, it hardly seems possible to reduce the history
of God's relationship with his people to a covenant of
grace. Abraham and David witness to an "everlasting covenant" fulfilled solely by Yahweh's unconditional resolve,
while the Sinaitic covenant was intended in the first place
as a temporary, transitional order anticipating the eschatological kingdom of God throughout the whole earth.
The covenant of grace is uninterrupted from Adam after
the fall to the present, while the Sinai Pact, conditional
and typological, has now become obsolete (Heb. 8:13),
its mission having been fulfilled (Gal. 3:23–4:7).

The apostle Paul was not an antinomian. That is, he was not
opposed to the law. To the contrary, he upheld the law, and his gospel heralded the amazing fact that through Christ's obedient life,
sacrificial death, and glorious resurrection and ascension, God had
remained both "just and the justifier of the one who has faith in Jesus"
(Rom. 3:26 NKJV). So it was not the law as law that troubled Paul.
"On the contrary, I would not have known sin except through the
law. . . . Therefore the law is holy, and the commandment holy and
just and good" (Rom. 7:7, 12 NKJV). The law is not the problem; I
am (vv. 13–24), so the only way of reconciliation and obtaining the
blessing is "through Jesus Christ our Lord!" (v. 25 NKJV).

Carriers of the legalistic virus in Galatia and elsewhere were
not faulted for having a positive view of the law, but for failing to
recognize that its purpose was to lead God's people to Christ. By
seeking to attain the everlasting promise of life *through* the temporal
and conditional covenant of law, Paul's opponents were actually
excommunicating themselves from the true Israel. Not only their
explicit sins but their confidence in their own obedience revealed
that they were "cut off" from the only one in whom they could be
found acceptable. For them, at least, Sinai could only be the emblem

of the condemnation that awaits them, since to be "under the law" is (for those who violate it) equivalent to being cursed (Gal. 3:10).

While the principles of law and promise agree on a number of points, they reflect intrinsically different types of covenants. Personal obedience to commands is a radically different basis for an inheritance than faith in a promise. While the Scriptures uphold the moral law as the abiding way *of* life for God's redeemed people, it can never be a way *to* life. Every covenant has two parties, and we assume the responsibilities of faithful partners, but the basis of acceptance with God is the covenant-keeping of another, the Servant of the Lord; and because of his faithfulness, we now inherit all of the promises through faith alone, as children of Sarah and citizens of the heavenly Jerusalem.

The new covenant announced by the prophets long ago included both justification *and* rebirth, imputed *and* imparted righteousness, forgiveness of sins *and* a new heart that thirsts for God and his glory. Yet, as we saw in Jeremiah 31, the second side of the coin (a new heart) is the result of the first (justification and forgiveness of sins). As Paul warns, we do not receive justification and forgiveness by grace alone, through faith alone, because of Christ alone, and then go on to sanctification as a matter of personal achievement (Gal. 3:1–4). In the new covenant, all of the blessings have Christ and his obedience as the only ground qualifying us as heirs. Not some of the blessings, but all of them, are comprehended "in Christ." This spells the end of both legalism and antinomianism: none of the blessings are the result of our own achievement, and at the same time, those who inherit the blessing of justification are equally beneficiaries of regeneration and sanctification. While our status before God (justification) is distinguished from our inward renewal (rebirth and sanctification), our status cannot be separated from our inward renewal even for a moment. Thus, because of God's sworn oath by himself, the justified sinner will also be one who perseveres against doubt, temptation, the world, the flesh, and the devil, one day inheriting by that same royal grant rest from all warfare.

5

From Scripture to System

The Heart of Covenant Theology

A T I T S B E S T, systematic theology never imposes a system
on Scripture but seeks instead to draw out the main teachings of Scripture from Scripture itself. At this point, I hope it
is clear that Scripture itself requires us to distinguish between
two types of covenant: unconditional and conditional. With the
help of even some non-Reformed Old Testament scholars, we
have seen the differences between the sort of oath God swears
by himself to Adam and Eve after the fall, to Noah, to Abraham
and Sarah, to David and his descendants, and the new covenant
on one side and the conditional works-principle explicitly set
forth in the Sinai covenant. This chapter moves into the heart of
systematic-theological territory, relating our biblical-theological
development of this theme to the traditional Reformed concept of
three overarching covenants: the covenant of redemption (an eternal pact between the Father, Son, and Holy Spirit), the covenant
of creation (made with humanity in Adam), and the covenant of
grace (made with believers and their children in Christ).

Three Overarching Biblical Covenants

Sometimes covenant theology is also called *federal* theology because of its emphasis on solidarity in a representative head. A representative system of government is called "federal," and Scripture calls us to see ourselves not simply as individuals but as those who are either "in Adam" or "in Christ."

A broad consensus emerged in this Reformed (federal) theology with respect to the existence in Scripture of three distinct covenants: the covenant of redemption (*pactum salutis*), the covenant of creation (*foederus naturae*), and the covenant of grace (*foederus gratiae*).[1] The other covenants in Scripture (Noahic, Abrahamic, Mosaic, Davidic) are all grouped under these broader arrangements. In the distinction between the covenant of works and the covenant of grace, we will recognize the conclusions of our previous chapters concerning law and gospel, conditionality and unconditionality, inheritance by personal performance of stipulations and inheritance by another's performance, received through faith in the promise. Before we attend to these two covenants worked out by God in history, however, let us look at another that stands behind all others.

1. The Covenant of Redemption

Most biblical covenants are historical pacts God has made with creatures. The covenant of redemption, however, is an eternal pact between the persons of the Trinity. The Father elects a people in the Son as their mediator to be brought to saving faith through the Spirit. Thus, this covenant made by the Trinity in eternity already takes the fall of the human race into account. Chosen out of the condemned mass of humanity, the elect are no better or no more qualified than the rest. God has simply chosen according to his own freedom to display both his justice and his mercy, and the covenant of redemption is the opening act in this drama of redemption.

Already we can see how such a covenantal framework challenges the idea of a solitary despot. The Father elects a people in the Son through the Spirit. Our salvation, therefore, arises first of all out of the joint solidarity of the divine persons. The joy of giving and receiving experienced by the Father, Son, and Holy Spirit spills over, as it were, into the Creator-creature relationship. In the covenant of redemption, the love of the Father and the Spirit for the Son is demonstrated in the gift of a people who will have him as their living head. At the same time, the Son's love for the Father and the Spirit is demonstrated in his pledge to redeem that family at the greatest personal cost.

This is why we are not to search out God's secret decree of predestination or to try to find evidence of it in ourselves, but, as Calvin urged, to see Christ as the "mirror" of our election. God's predestination is hidden to us, but Christ is not. The unveiling of the mystery hidden in past ages, the person and work of Christ, becomes the only reliable testimony to our election. Those who trust in Christ belong to Christ, are elect in Christ.

So far I have offered some definitions, but I have not yet offered any biblical defense. Is this covenant of redemption produced by theological speculation or careful biblical interpretation?

In answer to this question, we first should note that some contemporary Reformed theologians have suggested that Scripture is silent about such an eternal covenant. Yet these same writers affirm the traditional Reformed doctrine of election: God has chosen many from Adam's condemned race to be in Christ, apart from anything in or foreseen in those chosen and according to God's free grace alone. If we hold simultaneously to the doctrine of the Trinity and unconditional election, it is unclear what objection could be raised in principle to describing this divine decree in terms of the concept of an eternal covenant between the persons of the Godhead. Second, we are not left to arguments from silence. In the ministry of Christ, for example, the Son is represented (particularly in the fourth Gospel) as having been given a people by the Father (John 6:39; 10:29; 17:2, 4–10; Eph. 1:4–12; Heb.

2:13, citing Isa. 8:18) who are called and kept by the Holy Spirit for the consummation of the new creation (Rom. 8:29–30; Eph. 1:11–13; Titus 3:5; 1 Peter 1:5). In fact, to affirm the covenant of redemption is little more than affirming that the Son's self-giving and the Spirit's regenerative work were the execution of the Father's eternal plan. Not only were we chosen in Christ "before the foundation of the world" (Eph. 1:4 NKJV); Christ himself is spoken of as "the Lamb slain from the foundation of the world" (Rev. 13:8 KJV).

The covenant of redemption underscores not only God's sovereignty and freedom in electing grace, but the trinitarian and, specifically, Christ-centered character of that divine purpose. It all takes place "in Christ"; hence, the emphasis in covenant theology on the theme of "Christ the mediator." Even before creation and the fall, the elect were "in Christ" in terms of the divine purpose for history, though not yet *in history* itself. Far from being the result of abstract speculation, this concept of the covenant of redemption is both a revealed teaching of Scripture and the best guard against such speculation. Wherever God's sovereignty in predestination is strongly defended apart from such a covenantal framework, the concrete revelation of our election in Christ according to the promise of the gospel is often surrendered to theoretical debates that lead us into endless speculation on God's hidden counsels.

Despite this past consensus, Reformed theologians in our day are not unanimously persuaded that the eternal decree can be formalized as a *covenant* on the basis of exegesis. O. Palmer Robertson, for example, acknowledges the eternal decree.

> But affirming the role of redemption in the eternal counsels of God is not the same as proposing the existence of a pre-creation covenant between Father and Son. A sense of artificiality flavors the effort to structure in covenantal terms the mysteries of God's eternal counsels. Scripture simply does not say much on the pre-creation shape of the decrees of God. To speak concretely of an intertrinitarian [*sic*] "covenant" with terms and conditions between Father and Son mutually endorsed before the founda-

tion of the world is to extend the bounds of scriptural evidence beyond propriety.[2]

Further, how could a "sovereign disposition" be true in the case of the Trinity?[3]

Here again we see the dangers inherent in too narrow a definition of *covenant*. In the passages cited above, it would seem clear that the persons of the Trinity were engaged in a "pretemporal" disposition of some kind: the election of a people given to the Son as mediator to be preserved by the Spirit. In those passages especially in John's Gospel, Jesus speaks repeatedly of "[those] whom You [the Father] have given Me" (e.g., 17:6, 9, 11, 12 NKJV). The very notion of soteriological mediation requires some sort of pledge arrangement. In fact, it is precisely this trinitarian covenant that is able to counter a hyper-Calvinistic tendency toward a unitarian soteriology in which "God" (i.e., the Father) sovereignly decrees salvation and reprobation apart from the working of the Son and the Spirit. A trinitarian soteriology emerges necessarily out of this emphasis. "Just as the blessedness of God exists in the free relationship of the three Persons of the adorable Being, so man shall also find his blessedness in the covenantal relationship with God," writes Vos.[4]

Part of the difficulty for interpreters is that these passages do not specifically identify the decree as a covenant. Yet, as we have seen, the Davidic covenant was only acknowledged as such by the prophets much later (Psalm 89 and 132). Despite his accusation that this doctrine of a covenant of redemption is speculative, Robertson himself introduces heretofore unheard-of covenants. In addition to the Noahic, Abrahamic, Mosaic, and Davidic covenants, he adduces a "covenant of commencement" (with postlapsarian Adam) and a "covenant of consummation" (Christ), neither of which is identified explicitly as a covenant in Scripture. Scripture, to be sure, knows of no suzerain-vassal type of treaty between the persons of the Trinity. After all, each person is equally divine: there are no lords and servants in the eternal trinitarian relationship.

Furthermore, there is no formal treaty structure to this covenant in Scripture—no historical prologue, stipulations, sanctions, and so forth. But we have seen that not all biblical covenants fit this suzerainty type. Only an overly restrictive definition of covenant would seem to justify the claim that the covenant of redemption is speculative rather than biblical.

The covenant of redemption, therefore, is as clearly revealed in Scripture as the Trinity and the eternal decree to elect, redeem, call, justify, sanctify, and glorify a people for the Son. At the same time, this eternal purpose would have remained utterly hidden from us unless it had actually been realized in our time and space. That is where most of the biblical attention is given. While the covenant of redemption is eternal and has for its partners the persons of the Godhead, the covenants of creation and grace unfold in human history and have both Creator and creature as their partners.

One of the most succinct statements of this scheme of the two historical covenants is found in the seventh chapter of the Westminster Confession of Faith:

> The distance between God and the creature is so great, that although reasonable creatures do owe obedience unto him as their Creator, yet they could never have any fruition of him, as their blessedness and reward, but by some voluntary condescension on God's part, which he hath been pleased to express by way of covenant. The first covenant made with man was a covenant of works, wherein life was promised to Adam, and in him to his posterity, upon condition of perfect and personal obedience. Man, by his Fall, having made himself incapable of life by that covenant, the Lord was pleased to make a second, commonly called the covenant of grace: wherein he freely offered unto sinners life and salvation by Jesus Christ, requiring of them faith in him, that they may be saved, and promising to give unto all those that are ordained unto life, his Holy Spirit, to make them willing and able to believe.

2. The Covenant of Creation (Works)

Founded in creation itself, the covenant made initially between God and his viceroy has been variously labeled the covenant of creation, nature, law, and works. All of these terms are appropriate, as I contend below. This pact presupposes a righteous and holy human servant entirely capable of fulfilling the stipulations of God's law. It promises blessing on the basis of obedience and curse upon transgression. It pertains to humanity in a state of unblemished nature, not in a state of grace. However, I have chosen to use the term covenant of *creation* because it is the least controversial and most broadly useful.

If the covenant of redemption remains controversial, the so-called covenant of creation as a *covenant of works* is more still, especially in contemporary Reformed theology. I will allow some of the tradition's most exemplary representatives to define the position. According to Johannes Cocceius (1603–69),

> man who comes upon the stage of the world with the image of God, exists under a law and a covenant, and that a covenant of works. . . . When further we say that he who bears the image of God given in creation was established under God's covenant, we do not mean that he has a right to the communion and friendship of God, but that he is in that state in which he ought to ask the right to the communion and friendship of God and to make it stable and so to have the offer of God's friendship, if he obeys His law.[5]

This covenantal arrangement is "God's pact with Adam in his integrity, as the head of the whole human race, by which God requiring of man the perfect obedience of the law of works promised him if obedient eternal life in heaven, but threatened him if he transgressed with eternal death; and on his part man promised perfect obedience to God's requirement (Heidegger IX, 15)."[6]

The point that this covenant was made "with Adam in his integrity" is crucial. Prior to the fall, humanity in Adam was neither *sinful* nor *confirmed* in righteousness. He was on trial:

would he follow his covenant Lord's pattern of working and resting, subduing and reigning, or would he go his own way and seek
his own good apart from God's Word? Created for obedience,
he was entirely capable of maintaining himself in a state of integrity. Therefore, it is anachronistic to require grace or mercy
as the foundation of creation and covenant in the beginning, as
Karl Barth and many recent Reformed theologians do. "Law"
was not some external code, a list of dos and don'ts that stood
over against humanity; it was the reflection of God's own moral
character, which he was determined to share analogically with
his human partner.

   Law and love go hand in hand in Scripture. To obey God is to
love him, and if one wants to know how to love God, the answer
the Bible clearly gives is the law. Far from arbitrary, that law is the
expression of God's very being. It is not an impersonal legal code,
but the concrete revelation of that moral nature with which we
were created as God's image-bearers. When we hear the divine
benediction on the creation of humanity, "It is very good," we
are meant to see that here God saw himself in the mirror. The
law was natural not only for God, but for his image-bearer. The
difference was that while God cannot transgress his own moral
character, since he is *necessarily* holy and righteous, creatures are
only *contingently* so. Just as they exist as dependent creatures,
their holiness and righteousness depend on their determination to fulfill their "chief end," namely, "to glorify God and enjoy
him forever" (Westminster Shorter Catechism, Question and
Answer 1).

   The concept of a covenant of creation (works) reaches confessional status in the Westminster Confession, as I have mentioned, and is everywhere presupposed in the Canons of Dort. The
basic elements of the covenant of creation can even be discerned
in Augustine's claim: "The first covenant was this, unto Adam:
'Whensoever thou eatest thereof thou shalt die the death,'" and
this is why all his children "are breakers of God's covenant made
with Adam in paradise."[7] Irenaeus, too, anticipated the central

premises of the federal theologians on this point and clearly recognized the difference between the "covenant of law" and the "covenant of grace."[8]

While we should not be surprised to discover refinement and a variety of opinions on specific details, the contrast between Calvin and his later interpreters cannot be sustained. That is to say, the broad lines of the reformer's thought were refined and developed rather than distorted by his theological successors. In fact, the architects of federal theology clearly recognized that their covenant of works–grace scheme arose from their prior commitment to the distinction between law and gospel. As early as the first page of his *Commentary on the Heidelberg Catechism*, Zacharias Ursinus (primary author of the Heidelberg Catechism and formative federal theologian) states, "The doctrine of the church is the entire and uncorrupted doctrine of the law and gospel concerning the true God, together with his will, works, and worship."[9]

> The doctrine of the church consists of two parts: the Law, and the Gospel; in which we have comprehended the sum and substance of the sacred Scriptures.... Therefore, the law and gospel are the chief and general divisions of holy Scriptures, and comprise the entire doctrine comprehended therein ... for the law is our schoolmaster, to bring us to Christ, constraining us to fly to him, and showing us what that righteousness is, which he has wrought out, and now offers unto us. But the gospel, professedly, treats of the person, office, and benefits of Christ. Therefore we have, in the law and gospel, the whole of the Scriptures comprehending the doctrine revealed from heaven for our salvation.... The law prescribes and enjoins what is to be done, and forbids what ought to be avoided: whilst the gospel announces the free remission of sin, through and for the sake of Christ.... The law is known from nature; the gospel is divinely revealed.... The law promises life upon the condition of perfect obedience; the gospel, on the condition of faith in Christ and the commencement of new obedience.[10]

Calvin's successor in Geneva, Theodore Beza, made precisely
the same point in his *Confession*—adding the warning that "ig-
norance of this distinction between Law and Gospel is one of the
principle sources of the abuses which corrupted and still corrupt
Christianity."[11] William Perkins, father of Elizabethan Puritanism,
taught practical theology to generations of preachers through his
Art of Prophesying (1592). In that work he asserts:

> The basic principle in application is to know whether the passage
> is a statement of the law or of the gospel. For when the Word
> is preached, the law and the gospel operate differently. The law
> exposes the disease of sin, and as a side-effect stimulates and stirs
> it up. But it provides no remedy for it. . . . The law is, therefore,
> first in the order of teaching; then comes the gospel.[12]

Continental and British Reformed traditions are agreed in their
insistence upon this distinction, and it was strengthened rather
than abandoned as federal theology became increasingly refined.
This pattern of rendering "law-gospel" and "covenant of works–
covenant of grace" interchangeable continues all the way up to
Louis Berkhof's *Systematic Theology*, under the heading "The Two
Parts of the Word of God Considered as a Means of Grace."[13]

Geerhardus Vos defended the importance of the covenant of
works as part of the very essence of Reformed thought. First,
"covenant" is very important early on—not, as Heinrich Heppe
said (and later corrected), from Melanchthon, but from Zwingli
and Bullinger contra Anabaptists, although some Lutherans have
found the idea important.[14] With Luther, the Reformed have
sought to distinguish law and gospel in a way that any type of
synergism (i.e., salvation as a process of divine-human cooperation) is avoided in our understanding of justification and rebirth:
"Whatever has grown in synergistic soil cannot bear any healthy
Reformed fruits."[15]

This applies also to the covenant of works. Noting a growing tide of sentiment against the covenant of works, Vos replies

with great evidence that this too is from early days and enjoyed a wide consensus across the Reformed family: British, as well as Continental. We should "have no difficulty in recognizing the covenant of works as an old Reformed doctrine," with Ursinus's *Larger Catechism* as an example. "The doctrine of the covenant of works is found in the ninth question. The contrast of law and gospel is brought to bear on the contrast between the covenant of works and the covenant of grace."[16] It is in the Reformed doctrine of the covenant of works that God's glory, the original rectitude of humanity in creation, and the imputation of Christ's active as well as passive obedience can be maintained.[17] "If we are not mistaken, the instinctive aversion which some have to the covenant of works springs from a lack of appreciation for this wonderful truth."[18] Interestingly, Vos also sees a close connection between the eternal covenant of redemption and the temporal covenant of creation:

> It was merely the other side of the doctrine of the covenant of works that was seen when the task of the Mediator was also placed in this light. A *Pactum Salutis*, a Counsel of Peace, a Covenant of Redemption, could then be spoken of. There are two alternatives: one must either deny the covenant arrangement as a general rule for obtaining eternal life, or, granting the latter, he must also regard the gaining of eternal life by the Mediator as a covenant arrangement and place the establishing of a covenant in back of it. Thus it also becomes clear how a denial of the covenant of works sometimes goes hand in hand with a lack of appreciation for the counsel of peace.[19]

With the covenant of redemption, in which the Son is made the mediator of the elect, and the covenant of creation (or works), under which terms the Son, acting as mediator and second Adam, won eternal life under the law, "earning eternal life has forever been taken out of his [man's] hands. . . . On this point, the entire Reformation, both Lutheran and Calvinist, took exception to Rome, which failed to appreciate this fundamental truth."[20] In other words, the covenant of redemption contrasts the salvation of the elect to *Christ's* meritorious fulfillment of personal obedience to God's law.

Although this view of things is hardly representative of a fully developed federal theology, Calvin does assert the main features of the covenant of creation.[21] In a number of places, Calvin refers to Christ's having "merited" salvation for his people by his obedience, once more emphasizing the satisfaction of law as a necessary prerequisite for everlasting life.[22]

By no means are these distinct covenants (redemption, creation, grace) to be seen in chronological terms. This is the tendency of approaches in which the Old Testament is identified as "law" and the New Testament as "gospel." Nor are the principles of "law" and "promise"—when applied either to the original covenant of creation or its republication at Sinai—to be given merely negative and positive connotations, respectively, as if they are static categories of damnation and justification. In creation (and in the institution of the theocracy at Sinai), law as the basis for the divine-human relationship is wholly positive. In fact, this republication of the law is itself *gracious*, even if the principle of the two covenants (works and grace) fundamentally differs.

The error is in reading Paul's polemic against "law" (contrasted with "promise") as (1) a problem with "law" per se (e.g., Bultmann, Kasemann, et al.) and therefore (2) reading into all accounts of law covenants the indictment of "legalism." No one will be justified by "works of the law," according to Paul, not because there has never been an arrangement in which that was possible (i.e., creation), but because since the fall (which the history of Israel recapitulates), all of humanity (including Israel) is now "in Adam." The direct problem is not being under the law, but being found "in Adam," a transgressor of the law. But can one be legitimately sentenced under a law unless the stipulations and sanctions were clearly present and understood? And can this be seen as anything but a covenant?

The federal theologians founded this notion exegetically in two ways: first, by connecting the definition of a "covenant" with the admittedly sparse details of the Genesis narrative; second, by observing the references to such a natural arrangement in various subsequent texts.

As to the first way, it was argued that every covenant in Scripture is constituted by a series of formulae, most notably, oaths taken by both parties with stipulations and sanctions (blessings and curses). These elements appear to be present, albeit implicitly, in the creation narrative. Adam is created in a state of integrity with the ability to render God complete obedience, thus qualifying as a suitable human partner. Further, God commands such complete obedience, and he promises, upon that condition, the *right* (not the *gift*) to eat from the Tree of Life. While creation itself is a gift, the entrance into God's Sabbath rest was held out as the promise for loyal obedience in the period of testing.

As further confirmation, the presence of the Sabbath at the end of the six-day workweek (probation) holds out the promise of everlasting confirmation in blessedness. If Adam should default in this covenantal relationship, he would "surely die," and we learn from the subsequent failure of Adam that this curse brought in its wake not only spiritual, but physical, interrelational, and indeed environmental disaster. When we include references from the rest of Scripture, Adam is clearly seen not simply as an individual, but as a public representative. Not only was he in covenant with God, but all of humanity is represented as being in covenant with God by virtue of participating federally in Adam. If Adam was our covenant head, then this arrangement can only be characterized as a covenant. Indeed, all of creation was in some sense judged in Adam (Gen. 3:17–18; Rom. 8:20). It is with this simultaneously legal and relational background in mind that Paul makes his well-known statements on the imputation of Adam's sin as the corollary of the imputation of the second Adam's righteousness (especially Romans 5).[23]

In addition, the literary elements of covenant-making seem to be present in the Genesis narrative, especially as interpreted by the rest of Scripture. Even in Genesis 1–3 we recognize the features of a covenant that we have delineated: a historical prologue setting the stage (Genesis 1–2), stipulations (2:16–17), and sanctions (2:17b) over which Eve and the serpent argue (3:1–5) and which are finally carried out in the form of judgment (3:8–19). It is only after this fateful decision that an entirely new and unexpected basis is set forth for human destiny (3:21–24).[24]

Additional texts besides Genesis 1–3 appear to take into account just such an arrangement. Peter Van Mastricht, for example, quite typically appeals to Hosea 6:7, where it is said of Israel, "Like 'adam, they have broken the covenant" (cf. Job 31:33, where "as Adam did" is the most likely translation). As a theocracy typological of the eschatological paradise of God, Israel's *national* existence was a repetition of the covenant of creation—hence, the comparisons drawn by the biblical writers to Adam and the original creation.[25] Israel was called to see itself as the kingdom of God, a new garden of God's presence and a new creation in the sense of representing humanity before God—all of this typological of the true Israel, the faithful *Adam*, who is also the true heavenly temple and everlasting Sabbath of God.

As with Adam, the Sinaitic covenant made with Moses is conditional. If Israel is faithful, the people "may live long in the land the Lord [their] God is giving [them]" (Exod. 20:12 NIV). Thus, Israel's tenure in the land, like Adam's, is conditional—although in both cases (i.e., original creation and the giving of the land), God's goodness preceded the covenant-making. Precisely the same terms and sanctions apply. As with his appeal to the two Adams for the imputation of original sin and justification, Paul, as we have seen, draws on the analogy of two mountains and two mothers to contrast the covenant of works (law) and the covenant of grace (promise) (Galatians 3 and 4).

But for our purposes here, it is important to notice, as Mastricht points out, that the principle of works is strenuously maintained in Scripture. The "works of the law" demand "most punctilious obedience ('cursed is the man who does not do all the works therein')."

Only in this context, says Mastricht, can we possibly understand the role of Jesus Christ as the "fulfiller of all righteousness."

> Heb. 2.14–15 (since the children are sharers in blood and flesh, he also in like manner partook of the same; that through death he might bring to nought him that hath the power of death, that is, the devil). . . . If you say the apostle is speaking of a covenant not in Paradise, but the covenant at Sinai, the answer is easy, that the Apostle is speaking of the covenant in Paradise so far as it is reenacted and renewed with Israel at Sinai in the Decalogue, which contained the proof of the covenant of works.[26]

A further argument, says Mastricht, is the following:

> Synonyms of the covenant of works are extant in the NT: Rom. 3.27 (where is the glory? It is excluded. By what manner of law? Of works? Nay: but by a law of faith) Gal. 2.16 (knowing that a man is not justified by the works of the law save through faith in Jesus Christ . . . because by the works of the law shall no flesh be justified).[27]

If one objects that these passages merely demonstrate the opposite conclusion—that is, that one cannot be justified in a covenant of works—these theologians reply that it is only humanity after the fall—that is, sinful humanity—that cannot be justified by works. Adam, however, was in a state of rectitude, perfectly capable of acceding to the divine mandate. As created, Adam and Eve's delight was to do the will of God.

To refuse *in principle* the possibility of Adam's fulfillment of the covenant of works is to challenge the original state of integrity.[28] In addition to the exegetical arguments, Mastricht adduces the intrasystematic importance of the doctrine.

> To very many heads of the Christian religion, e.g., the propagation of original corruption, the satisfaction of Christ and his subjection to divine law: Rom. 8.3–4 (what the law could not do, in

that it was weak through the flesh, God, sending his own Son in the likeness of sinful flesh and for sin, condemned sin in the flesh, that the requirement of the law might be fulfilled in us, who walk not after the flesh, but after the Spirit); Gal. 3:13 (Christ redeemed us from the curse of the law, having become a curse for us . . .), we can scarcely give suitable satisfaction, if the covenant of works be denied.[29]

Olevianus, coauthor of the Heidelberg Catechism, sees in the original covenant's prohibition the essence of the whole law—love of God and neighbor.[30] And in this state Adam could expect—for himself and his covenant heirs—royal entrance into the consummation, the Sabbath rest of God himself, and everlasting confirmation in righteousness. In the words of the Formula Consensus Helvetica, "the promise annexed to the covenant of works was not just the continuation of earthly life and felicity," but of a confirmation in righteousness and everlasting heavenly joy.[31]

A final argument in favor of the covenant of creation is supplied by Cocceius, in terms natural to one influenced by Calvin's thought: the argument from *conscience*. By nature human beings know that they have offended God's friendship and communion. All of this presupposes an original relationship that has been breached.[32] According to Cocceius, we know this is a real covenant from (1) the conscience (Rom. 2:15), (2) the longing for eternal life, (3) the "daily and continual benefits by which man is urged to seek his Creator and Benefactor and to love, glorify and thank Him."[33] Every human being is aware not only of God's existence, but of God's righteous commandments, which he or she suppresses in unrighteousness. Where did this awareness come from? How can an obligation to a person exist unless a prior relationship existed, and how can one be judged—even condemned, apart from any specific law that one has knowingly breached?

However, Scripture nowhere presupposes a universal knowledge of the gospel. The law is universal because it is natural: we are simply "wired" for it. It belongs to us by nature in creation, while the gospel is an announcement of good news in the event of transgression. It has to be preached, whereas the law belongs to the conscience of every person already. Therefore, the original relationship of humanity to God is one of law and love, not of grace and mercy. It is therefore premature to insert into the creation covenant an element of divine graciousness, strictly speaking. To be sure, God's decision and act to create is a "voluntary condescension" (Westminster Confession of Faith 7.1), as is his entrance into a covenantal relationship with his human creatures. Nevertheless, if grace is to retain its force as divine clemency toward those who deserve condemnation, we are wiser to speak of divine wisdom, goodness, justice, and righteousness as the governing characteristics of creation. Grace and mercy are shown to covenant-breakers and reflect the divine commitment to restore that which is fallen.

It is within this framework, then, that Reformed orthodoxy understood the active obedience of Jesus Christ, emphasizing the significance of his humanity in achieving redemption for his covenant heirs.[34] His active obedience refers to the thirty-three years of perfectly obeying the Father in order to "fulfill all righteousness" (Matt. 3:15; 5:17 NRSV). The priority of law in the covenant of creation establishes the fact that God cannot acquit the guilty; nor can he simply forgive sinners. In the context of the covenant of creation, the law must be perfectly satisfied, either personally or representatively. To reflect God as his image-bearer is therefore to be righteous, holy, obedient—a covenant servant, defined as such by the covenant charter (Hos. 6:7, with Isa. 24:5; Jer. 31:35–37; 33:20–22, 25–26).

Thus all humans are created in God's image—and remain so, in fact, after the fall—precisely because they are *ex pacto* participants in the covenant of creation by their very existence. To be created in God's image is to be in covenant with God. Though vitiated by human rebellion, this covenant is still in effect. One is either "under the law" or "under grace"—that is, bound to either the covenant of creation (Adam) or the covenant of grace

(Christ). After the fall, any positive act of God toward human beings can be considered gracious. From his preservation of Cain to his providence in the secular nation-states of our day, God restrains his wrath as well as the effects of sin and even endows the wicked with good things in his common grace. Yet the terms for reconciliation with God remain in effect: under the covenant of creation, all are under a curse. Whatever gracious support God gives in this life to those who remain "in Adam," the final judgment will be according to works and entire perfection will be the only acceptable standard.

Israel's story recapitulates Adam's creation and fall. Like Adam, Israel is placed in a beautiful garden they did not make, with God's Sabbath enthronement held out as the prize for faithful stewardship in the land. Therefore, Israel's probation pointed to Christ in two ways: by reiterating the inability of humanity to fulfill the law because of sin and by establishing ceremonies, sacrifices, a temple, a kingship, and a priesthood as shadows of the Coming One, the true and faithful Adam-Israel. It is he who, in his royal entrance, brings captives in his train, claiming the reward for his obedience for himself and for his coheirs. Thus, in him, law and gospel embrace without being confused; justice and grace are equally displayed without being synthesized.

This account provides the soil for a robust notion of the humanity of Christ. God alone could not have saved us. Our Savior had to be the second Adam. Throughout his relatively brief messianic career, Jesus recapitulated Adam's testing in the garden and Israel's forty-year testing in his own forty-day probation in the desert and, in fact, the entirety of his life. On the basis of his having fulfilled the covenant of creation representatively (i.e., federally), he can now dispense his reward to us within a covenant of grace.

This doctrine of the creation covenant or "covenant of works" has been subjected to criticism not only by those outside of the Reformed tradition, but by many within it. However, as we have seen, the doctrine is vindicated by exegesis, and apart from it, a great deal in the biblical traditions is left inchoate. While few of the biblical scholars we have relied on in the previous chapter would have heard of, much less endorsed, a formal doctrine of the creation covenant as we have here, the labors especially since the middle of the last century have contributed to renewed possibilities for appreciating the doctrine's significance. Indeed, it is not always the case that a dogmatic formulation enjoys such unintended support from the guild of biblical studies. If biblical scholars are providing new grist for the covenantal mill, it may be time for systematic theology to catch up. Nearly a century ago Geerhardus Vos made this acknowledgment:

> For, although it is generally considered a dogmatic anachronism to carry the covenant-idea back into the original religious status of unfallen man, as the Reformed Theology has done in its doctrine of the covenant of works, a most striking confirmation of the biblical warrant for this view has of late come from an altogether unexpected quarter. No less a scholar than Wellhausen has observed that in P, the so-called priestly document, the ancient history is represented as determined in its onward movement by the four covenants which in succession God makes with man, whence also the name of "the four-covenant book" has come into use to designate the peculiar structure of this document. And as the first of these four covenants, it is maintained by Wellhausen and others, the author must have counted the arrangement entered into by God with our first parents in their original state. Thus the much ridiculed "covenant of works" has been exegetically rehabilitated and it has been shown that the Reformed theologians were not so utterly lacking in historic sense as their critics believed.[35]

O. Palmer Robertson sees more exegetical warrant for the covenant of creation than for the covenant of redemption. First, he cites the support of Jewish commentators who referred the original breaking of God's covenant not to the golden calf episode at Sinai, but "to the disobedience of Adam in the Garden of Eden."[36] "A bond of life and death clearly is present between God and man newly created (Gen. 2:15–17)," according to Robertson. "The presence of all elements essential to the existence of a covenant in these relationships of God to man prior to Noah provides adequate basis for the designation of these circumstances as 'covenantal.' Although the term 'covenant' may not appear, the essence of a covenantal relationship is certainly present."[37]

However, just at this point, Robertson is reticent to adopt a covenant of works–covenant of grace contrast, insisting (as John Murray) that grace is fundamental to any divine-human relationship and that works are required in any such arrangement as well. This ambivalence leads Robertson to confuse the principles of law and promise:"While salvation is by faith, judgment is by works."[38] How salvation is distinguished from judgment is not clear, but in Scripture the good news is that for the believer the verdict of the last judgment has already been rendered in the present: "no condemnation" (Rom. 8:1 NRSV). Robertson recognizes, "Paul contrasts the Abrahamic and the Mosaic periods of the Old Testament (Gal. 3:15–19). The apostle makes it plain that the inheritance of God's blessing is not based on law, but on promise. By such an antithesis, he sets the Mosaic covenant of law over against the Abrahamic covenant of promise." So far so good.

> Yet it must be recognized again that Paul's ultimate purpose in this entire discussion is to distance the true gospel of Christ from every approximation of the Judaizers' false gospel. His discussion focuses on law as isolated from promise and its fulfillment in Christ. Law under Moses never was intended to function apart from promise. *Separated from its promise-dimension, which reached its fulfillment in Christ, law never could provide a way for making sinners righteous.*[39]

But is it not the case that for Paul"law" never could provide a way for making sinners righteous even when linked to its promise dimension? Is it not the case that "what the *law* was powerless to do" because of human sin "God *did* by sending his own Son" (Rom. 8:3 NIV)?

Robertson is skeptical, therefore, of M. G. Kline's defense of the classic federal view, which identified Israel's national covenant (Sinai) with law (indeed, the republication of the covenant of creation), and personal election and salvation with the covenant of grace (Abraham). Once more, however, Kline's position is hardly idiosyncratic. Not only is it an elaboration of a significant Reformed consensus in the past, but it is supported by numerous studies in Hebrew covenants by scholars outside the Reformed tradition. If we begin with an a priori definition of covenant that requires grace, we will miss the sharp distinction between law and promise that we find in Scripture. Our concept of covenant must be broad enough to encompass the various examples that we find in Scripture; otherwise, our systematic-theological conclusions are determining rather than resulting from exegesis.

This leads us to the consideration of the controversial claim that the Mosaic economy (i.e., the Sinai covenant) represents a law covenant rather than a promise covenant—in other words, that it is a republication in some sense of the original covenant with Adam. It is one thing to acknowledge the biblical grounds for the covenant of creation as a works arrangement, but it is quite another to assert that this is the sort of covenant that the nation of Israel had with God in Palestine. What should we make of this?

Kline comments "that the Sinaitic covenant as such '. . . made inheritance to be by law, not by promise—not by faith, but by works.'"[40] Robertson misunderstands this position as holding out two ways of salvation, but Kline clearly distinguishes, as the theologians we have considered, between the way of salvation in the covenant of grace (in both testaments) and the way of national preservation in the land, which is clearly founded on national obedience. Robertson does admit that the Sinai covenant highlights our sin and self-trust. "In this respect, Sinai represents a covenantal administration in sharpest contrast with Abraham's promise-covenant."[41] If so, it is unclear why Robertson would be so reluctant to regard the Sinai covenant as different *in principle* from the Abrahamic and, consequently, to see the theocracy as a renewed law covenant, especially when there are so many parallels (the historical prologues, stipulations, sanctions, and even covenantal signs) between the creation covenant and Sinai.

Robertson does see exegetical warrant for the covenant of creation in the beginning. "Through this creating/speaking relationship, God established sovereignly a life-and-death bond. This original bond between God and man may be called the covenant of creation."[42] Further, the Noahic covenant, given its absolute and unconditional character (God alone promises), brings creation after the fall into closer relation to the covenant of grace and God's final goal for all of redeemed creation.

> The covenant with Noah emphasizes the close interrelation of the creative and redemptive covenants. Much of God's bond with Noah entails a renewal of the provisions of creation, and even reflects closely the language of the original covenant. The reference to the "birds . . . cattle . . . [and] creeping things" of Genesis 6:20 and 8:17 compares with the similar description in Genesis 1:24, 25, 30. God's charge to Noah and his family to "be fruitful, and multiply, and fill the earth" (Gen. 9:1, 7) reflects the identical command given at creation (Gen. 1:28).[43]

This is further substantiated by the *tolodot* sections: "The phrase 'these are the generations of . . .' which begins Genesis 6:9 occurs ten times in Genesis. Each time the phrase indicates the beginning of another major section of the book. This phrase decisively separates the statement that 'Noah found grace' (Gen. 6:8) from the affirmation that Noah was a 'righteous man' (Gen. 6:9)."[44] Further, families are included, as they are in the covenant of grace more generally: "'I will establish my covenant with you, and you will enter the ark—you and your sons and your wife and your sons' wives with you (Gen. 6:18).'"[45]

Similar to the self-maledictory oath that God swears unilaterally in the Abrahamic covenant (Genesis 15), the oath here in Genesis 8:20–22 includes a sign: the rainbow. As Kline notes, "'My bow' translates *qeset*, the usual meaning of which is the weapon. Thus, the recurring rainbow imposed on the retreating storm by the shining again of the sun is God's battle bow laid aside, a token of grace staying the lightning-shafts of wrath."[46] It is a "pledge to death," with the seed of the serpent crushed (Gen. 9:6) and the opportunity for the redemptive purposes of God to resume in the world.[47]

This rainbow appears in the new creation with the throne scene: "He who sat there had the appearance of jasper and carnelian, and around the throne was a rainbow that had the appearance of an emerald," with the twenty-four elders (the twelve tribes and twelve apostles) enthroned around the suzerain Yahweh (Rev. 4:3–4).

Robertson reminds us, "The Exodus narrative begins when God hears the groaning of Israel, and 'remembers his covenant with Abraham, with Isaac, and with Jacob' (Exod. 2:24)."[48] Thus, law is placed within the context of covenant rather than simply reducing the latter to the former. This is a crucial observation. At the same time, we must bear in mind that no text in the Law or the Prophets relates subsequent covenants to the Sinaitic in this way. While God's mercies to the Israelites despite their disloyalty to the Sinaitic covenant are always justified on the basis of the Abrahamic promise, there are no passages that read, "Yet God remained faithful to David/the house of David for the sake of his covenant with Moses and the people at Horeb." The covenant does not work in reverse. God never remains faithful to unfaithful national Israel on the basis of the Sinaitic covenant itself—for on that basis, as he repeatedly says, he would have scattered them long ago. And yet it *is* on the basis of the Sinaitic covenant that God *exiles* Judah and eventually, through Jesus's prophetic ministry, abolishes the theocracy and pronounces judgment upon it. This reiterates the fact that the ministry of Moses could not bring about that blessedness that was the positive side of the sanctions—not because it was flawed, but because those who answered with one voice, "We will do all these things," in fact did not.

Whatever correspondences can be made between the original covenant with Adam and the covenant with the tribes gathered at

Sinai, we ought not ignore the differences between the acceptance of Adam in a state of integrity and the election of Israel despite a lack of integrity (Deut. 7:7–8; 9:6). Brevard Childs reminds us:

> Israel became the people of God, not by a natural bond, but by its experience of redemption from Egypt which it understood as an act of divine favour. . . . According to Exodus 19:1–6 Israel's existence as a special possession is conditioned on her obedience to the covenant. Israel's status was not established on the basis of her obedience, but a disregard of the covenant obligations could call the relation into question.[49]

This is a good point also in regard to the Adamic covenant: it is not that Adam's obedience was the ground of his creation in God's image, yet there is a great difference between saying that God's creation of and special relationship to humankind before the fall was owing to divine *goodness*, and saying that God's election of Israel was an act of divine *grace*. Grace, on this account, presupposes a lack of integrity in the covenant partner. In fact, it presupposes a state of sin.

So it is a false dilemma to ask whether, for example, Paul has in mind law in general (obedience to commands) or conformity to the Mosaic administration—specifically, boundary markers such as dietary laws. Both are in view, as the latter is a distinctive of the former. Life does not come from the ministry of Moses simply because law has no inherent power to do anything more than command—even if it is God's own law. Not only some laws are in view: "But when the goodness and lovingkindness of God our Savior appeared, he saved us not because of any works of righteousness that we had done, but according to his mercy" (Titus 3:4–5 NRSV).

The Decalogue (Ten Commandments), although it begins with the indicative announcement of God's liberation—thus showing its continuity with the Abrahamic promise—is basically a law covenant. Purely a suzerainty treaty, it does not obligate God to do anything but instead simply commands, with sanctions for obedience and disobedience. If the Israelites, about to enter Canaan, obey God's will thus revealed, they will "live long in the land the LORD [their] God is giving [them]" (Exod. 20:12 NIV). They are not promised that they will inherit the heavenly rest, but only the earthly copy of that rest, and this is how the New Testament understands the relation of the earthly and heavenly Jerusalem. So it does not contradict the Abrahamic promise in the slightest. No one in the Old Testament obtained the inheritance by works, but only by promise. Yet Israel's national status in God's land depended on fulfillment of the treaty's terms.

As the Epistle to the Hebrews emphasizes, neither Abraham nor Joshua regarded the earthly inheritance as ultimate. Instead, they looked through this arrangement to the original promise of a heavenly rest. This also accords with Paul's insistence in Galatians that the later covenant cannot annul the earlier one. The principle of law is the basis for remaining in the earthly land; the principle of promise is the basis for entering and remaining in the heavenly land. In this way, we are preserved from two problems that result from a confusion of the land promise (law) and the everlasting Sabbath (gospel). The first problem (older dispensationalism) is to think of the Old Testament believer as one who sought to be justified by works, and the second (covenantal nomism) is to regard the conditions for preservation in the earthly land as conditions for enjoyment of everlasting life, either for the Israelites or for new covenant believers.

Israelites under the old covenant and believers under the new are justified by grace alone through faith alone because of Christ alone. The difference is the theocratic parenthesis of redemptive history in which the typological kingdom is front and center. But this tutelage gives way to adulthood when the reality appears in Christ, who not only fulfills the law in our place but pours out his Spirit on the true children of Abraham, Jew and Gentile. Thus, they are correct who insist upon the continuity of God's covenant of grace from Adam to Noah to Abraham to Moses to David to

Christ as to the terms of eternal blessedness in God's covenant. The continuity is between Old and New Testaments, not between the Abrahamic and Sinaitic covenants. The sharp contrasts drawn not only by the Protestant Reformers, but by Jeremiah, Jesus, Paul, and the writer to the Hebrews require us to do justice also to the differing goals and principles of the Abrahamic and Mosaic economies. The theocracy—the outward administration of the ministry of Moses, most closely identified with the old covenant—has only a typological continuity with the new covenant. It is the everlasting rest that alone constitutes the continuity of these Old Testament covenants that receive their fulfillment in Christ. Moses himself was deemed unworthy of entering God's temporal rest, while he was worthy in Christ of the everlasting rest.

The parallels abound and are too obvious to be unintended: Israel, "a land flowing with milk and honey," is God's garden to be cleansed from all "serpents" that would lead his people astray and threaten it as the dwelling place of Yahweh with his people. When the people are exiled, the land is reclaimed by thorns. Both begin with historical prologues: creation in the first case, new creation exodus in the other. Both have a conditional character, with the stipulations to listen to and follow Yahweh alone, with the sanctions of life for obedience and death for disobedience. "Do this and you shall live" is the principle of both (Lev. 18:5).

The sacrifices under the Mosaic economy, Robertson contends, show that this was not a works type of arrangement.[50] But, in fact, these sacrifices only demonstrate that, as Paul says (Gal. 3:17), the later covenant did not cancel the earlier one; that even though Israel as a corporate entity could remain in the land only as long as they obeyed, personal salvation was still the result of faith in the promise. "It is sometimes assumed that the covenant of law temporarily replaced the covenant of promise, or somehow ran alongside it as an alternative method of man's salvation," says Robertson.[51] However, there is no footnote for this assertion, and in fact, it would be very difficult to find a credible Reformed theologian, past or present, who holds this view. No Reformed writer I am aware of has argued that Old Testament believers were saved by works simply because their tenure in the land (typological of the heavenly reality, particularly of the true Israelite who would come down from heaven to keep the covenant faithfully) was dependent on corporate obedience. Robertson implies that Kline sees the law under Moses "as opening a new way of attaining salvation for God's people," but this is a serious misunderstanding of Kline's position.[52]

Clearly, law functioned before and after this covenant, so why is it distinctively styled a "law covenant"? First, it is considered a law covenant because it gives greater fullness to God's previously enunciated commands. There is a particular concentration on the duties required of God's covenant people in this section of the canon and in this period of redemptive history. Second, law is the basis for whatever is distinctive about this covenant. The words here are carefully chosen: the writer is not saying that the entire reality of God's dealings with his people during this epoch is controlled by the principle of law or founded on it rather than on promise, but that whatever is distinctive about the ministry of Moses relates to the earthly, national, temporal, transitory, shadowy, pedagogical—and that this is administered by law (foreshadowing the true Israel) rather than promise. Still, the very fact that the true Israel himself nevertheless fulfills "all that is written in the law to do them" demonstrates that individual believers and their seed—even during the theocratic epoch—inherit everlasting life according to a covenant of grace. Israel's covenant-breaking, no more than David's and his descendants', cannot annul God's promise to Abraham and his seed (and in him, us all).

Even N. T. Wright, a critic of Reformation biases in Pauline studies, observes the necessary distinction between commands and promises. "As later tradition put it, Abraham will be God's means of undoing the sin of Adam."[53]

> Except for [Gen.] 35.11f., echoed in 48.3f., the command ("be fruitful . . .") has turned into a promise ("I will make you fruitful . . .").

The word "exceedingly" is added in ch. 17. And, most importantly, possession of the land of Canaan, and supremacy over enemies, has taken the place of the dominion over nature given in 1.28. We could sum up this aspect of Genesis by saying: Abraham's children are God's true humanity, and their homeland is the new Eden.[54]

The Abrahamic and Mosaic covenants are related as the everlasting Sabbath rest is related to the typological rest in the land and on every seventh day. In fact, the Sabbath institution is a concrete instance of the double aspect: the outward observance is not dispensed with, but the inward sense of the Sabbath gains much greater clarity as it centers around Christ and his work for us (Isa. 61:1–3; cf. Luke 4:18–19).

Because the new covenant represents the fulfillment of the Abrahamic promise, one might say that it puts the law in its place. Therefore, Robertson observes:

> it is fitting that the new covenant radically alters the Sabbath perspective. The current believer in Christ does not follow the Sabbath pattern of the people of the old covenant. He does not first labor six days, looking hopefully toward rest. Instead, he begins the week by rejoicing in the rest already accomplished by the cosmic event of Christ's resurrection. Then he enters joyfully into his six days of labor, confident of success through the victory which Christ already has won.[55]

3. The Covenant of Grace

The third covenant in the federal scheme is the covenant of grace. Once the second Adam has successfully fulfilled this covenant ("For them I sanctify myself, that they too may be truly sanctified" [John 17:19 NIV]), the benefits of this feat are dispersed by the Spirit according to a *gracious* covenant. Thus, the terms of the divine benediction here are reversed. Instead of acknowledging the inherent goodness, truth, and beauty of sinners, Jesus pronounces them just on the basis of the inherent justice of another (*iustitia alienum*). It is a true judgment rather than a legal fiction because the requisite covenantal righteousness is indeed fully present in the covenantal head (by fulfilling the creation covenant) and therefore belongs to his body by incorporation.

Like the covenant of creation, this covenant is made between God and human partners—in this case, fallen Adam, Seth, Abraham, and David. It is in this covenant that provisions are made for offenders, based on another's fulfillment of the legal covenant on their behalf. Thus, instead of it being a covenant based on law ("Do this and you shall live"), it is based on promise ("Live and you will do this"). There are real partners in this covenant (God with believers and their children) and real conditions (repentance and faith), but as it is grounded in the eternal covenant of redemption and the Mediator's fulfillment of the covenant of works, even the meeting of these conditions is graciously given and not simply required.

It is precisely this contrast that, according to the Reformed theologians, energizes so much of Pauline theology especially. Jesus is the faithful Israelite who fulfilled the covenant of works so that we could through his victory inherit the promises according to a covenant of grace. This gracious covenant is announced in Eden after the fall as the so-called *protoeuangelion* (Gen. 3:15). Eventually, God will call Abram out of the city of alienation and establish his covenant of grace with him, along with a provisional and thoroughly conditional covenant of works. The former covenant establishes the basis for the everlasting inheritance of the heavenly Jerusalem, while the latter establishes the terms of the temporal inheritance of the earthly Jerusalem as a typological reunion of cult and culture pointing forward to the reign of God in Christ. Abraham himself was looking through the temporal promises to the "city that has foundations, whose architect and builder is God" (Heb. 11:10 NRSV).

As far as the temporal land grant, Israel ("like Adam," Hos. 6:7) defiled the land, transgressed this conditional covenant, leading to their eviction from the new temple-garden of God, but once more the covenant of grace provided the terms of rescue for those who looked to the promise rather than the law for their redemption. The Abrahamic covenant rather than the Mosaic covenant establishes the terms of this arrangement. It is in this context that we better understand such passages as Jeremiah 31:32: "It will not be like the covenant I made with their forefathers when I took them by the hand to lead them out of Egypt" (NIV), and Galatians 3:17–18: "My point is this: the law, which came four hundred thirty years later, does not annul a covenant previously ratified by God, so as to nullify the promise. For if the inheritance comes from the law, it no longer comes from the promise; but God granted it to Abraham through the promise" (NRSV).

Thus, in the covenant of grace, God restores in his new creation what was lost in the old creation and could not be recovered according to the original principle that was established in nature. Because of the covenant of grace and the Messiah's having fulfilled the covenant of works, "The promise of entering his rest still stands" (Heb. 4:1; cf. v. 9).

Covenant theology has always therefore been eschatologically oriented, convinced that creation was the beginning rather than the goal of human existence. Humankind was created to pass through the probationary period and attain the right to eat from the Tree of Life. Thus, the telos of human existence was not fully present in creation, but was held out as a future reward. Humankind would lead creation in triumphal procession into the consummation, represented by the Tree of Life. Adam was to imitate God's sovereign session and, as a creature, climb the steps of eternal glory to claim his prize for himself and his posterity, and take his place as vassal king under the great Suzerain. Only in the fulfillment of the covenant of creation by the second Adam is the destiny of the image-bearer finally attained.

God's call to Abraham was "Leave your country, your people and your father's household" (Gen. 12:1 NIV). Similarly Jesus commanded his disciples to leave their nets and follow him. Whatever stipulations, whatever requirements and demands God puts on his people, they will never—can never—be the basis for his judgment of their status before him. Like the prologue to the Decalogue, the covenant of grace in every administration issues with a sovereign call simply to "come" on the basis of the liberation that has already occurred and is being announced. Since most of what follows in this work concentrates on the covenant of grace, I will let this brief account suffice.

Concluding Observations on the Covenants

Like much else in the Calvinistic system, a certain order makes one doctrine stand or fall on another. This may be the result of the imposition of a rigorous logic extraneous to the biblical text. Or, on the other hand, it may reflect the consistency of biblical and systematic claims. Regardless, each of these covenants stands or falls with the others. Especially in the light of church history, Vos's suspicion seems justified that a failure to adequately distinguish and maintain both the covenants of creation and grace, law and promise, eventually undermines the principle of *sola gratia* (grace alone).

On the other hand, as noted a theologian of *sola gratia* as Karl Barth regards the development of the covenant of works–covenant of grace scheme as a "fatal historical moment" in the Reformed tradition.[56] Barth rejected this formula at least in part because it distinguished grace as a post-fall phenomenon. He also sharply disagrees with the "introduction of an understanding of revelation as a sequence of stages," which "contributed to the historicization of revelation in later theology."[57] On both of these counts, however, the formulations of the older federal theology are worth reappraisal in view especially of some of the weaknesses that have been criticized in Barth's dogmatics.

In the light of our survey of Reformed covenant theology, Scripture is seen to be more emphatic that the original creation covenant is no more set aside than the law of Moses, but rather is fulfilled—not by us but by the one who was appointed mediator before the foundation of the world and has appeared in these last days, born under the law, to redeem those under the law."There is no gift that has not been earned by Him."[58]

> Rollock already demonstrates how the work of the Mediator with respect to the covenant of grace was nothing but a carrying through in him of the covenant of works broken in Adam. "Christ, therefore, our Mediator, subjected himself unto the covenant of works, and unto the law for our sake, and did both fulfill the condition of the covenant of works in his holy and good life . . . and also did undergo that curse with which man was threatened in that covenant of works, if that condition of good and holy works were not kept. . . . Wherefore we see Christ in two respects, to wit, in doing and suffering, subject to the covenant of works, and in both respects he has most perfectly fulfilled it, and that for our sake whose Mediator he is become (Rollock, *Works*, I, 52f)."[59]

The Anglican Puritan John Preston adds:

> It is said, "the promise is made to the Seed," yet the promise is made to us, and yet again the covenant is made with Abraham: How can all these stand together? Answer: The promises that are made to the Seed, that is to Christ himself, are these: Thou shalt be a priest forever; and I will give thee the kingdom of David; thou shalt sit on that throne; thou shalt be a prince of peace, and the government shall be upon thy shoulders; likewise, thou shalt be a prophet to my people. . . . These are the promises that are made to the Seed. The promises that are made to us, though they be of the same covenant, nevertheless differ in this respect: the active part is committed to the Messiah, to the Seed himself, but the passive part consists of the promises made to us: You shall be taught; you shall be made prophets; you shall have your sins forgiven. . . . So the promise is made to us. How is the promise made to Abraham? It reads, "In thee all the nations of the earth shall be blessed." The meaning is that they are derivative promises. The primary and original promises were made to Jesus Christ.[60]

As we have seen, many of these trajectories are at least anticipated by the ancient Christian writers.[61] Vos thinks the covenant
of redemption is the basis for the covenant of grace and insists that
this is the great Reformed consensus. "The covenant of redemption does not stand by itself, but is the basis of the economy of
salvation. It is the great prelude which in the Scriptures resounds
from eternity on into our own time and which we can already listen
to [in] the pure tones of the psalm of grace."[62] It is what keeps the
covenant of grace gracious, so to speak. It is the context in which
union with Christ obtains such clear identity.

As Reformed theologian Wilhelm Niesel pointed out, even
the third (normative) use of the law is supposed to lead us back
to Christ. Although "Reformed theology recognises the contrast
between Law and Gospel, in a similar way to Lutheranism," Niesel
adds, "law"—in its third use, as guidance in the Christian life—
now becomes adapted to the character of the covenant of grace.

> If we enjoy union with Christ, not only we ourselves but even our
> works too are just in God's sight. This doctrine of the justification
> of works (which was developed in the Reformed Church) is of the
> greatest consequence for ethics. It makes clear that the man who
> belongs to Christ need not be the prey of continual remorse. On the
> contrary he can go about his daily work confidently and joyfully.[63]

According to Vos, even the Reformed theologians "who strictly
separate law and gospel and make the latter to consist wholly of
promises—as a matter of fact, those theologians more than others—put emphasis on the fact that the law, as the comprehensive
norm for the life of man, also determines man's relation to the
gospel."[64] Interestingly, Vos notes that although the Sinaitic covenant should be seen as a republication of the covenant of works,
it is only such in the interests of holding out the promise of the
covenant of grace:

> When the work of the Spirit by means of the law and gospel leads
> to true conversion, in this conversion the longing for this lost

ideal of the covenant appears as an essential part. [We] can also explain why the older theologians did not always clearly distinguish between the covenant of works and the Sinaitic covenant. At Sinai it was not the "bare" law that was given, but a reflection of the covenant of works revived, as it were, in the interests of the covenant of grace continued at Sinai.[65]

Thus it is not only through the doctrine of justification that we are able to assure disquieted consciences that God is gracious to them, but on the wider basis of the Abrahamic covenant of grace. "The covenant is neither a hypothetical relationship, nor a conditional position; rather it is the fresh, living fellowship in which the power of grace is operative."[66] Not only at one point (justification), but from beginning to end, the relationship in which we stand before our God is founded on God's own oath, fulfilled in the work of his Son, made effective through the work of his Spirit. For Christ, by his personal fulfillment of the covenant of creation, has won for us the right to eat from the Tree of Life. The inheritance that he attained according to a covenant of law is now ours according to a covenant of promise. There simply is no better foundation for confidence and no richer source of daily comfort in life and in death.

6

Providence and Covenant

Common Grace

COVENANT HELPS US to see in our doctrine of providence the inseparable relation of God's sovereignty and human freedom—indeed, creaturely freedom in general. The pattern of creation, after all, is covenantal: the Great King speaks and the servant (stars, wind, land animals, birds, fish, mountains, rivers, oceans, and finally this marvel of ensouled dust, Adam) answers back faithfully. "'Let there be . . .!' And there was. . . ." This also fits the pattern of treaty-making. The great king would decree the terms of the treaty, and the servant would reply, "Here I am. Let it be done unto me according to your word." Two of the most basic points this yields are the following:

1. *God's speaking and our answering are not on the same level.* The Great King alone has the power to create *ex nihilo* (i.e., from nothing). The image-bearer cannot create its own image but can only reflect the original. There is not a common fund of freedom to be rationed by God and us, but rather the sort of freedom that

111

a sovereign, necessary, self-sufficient, uncaused Creator enjoys and the sort of freedom with which he endows dependent creatures in his image. As image-bearers, we are always analogies of God, not at any point identical. Our knowledge, freedom, and power are not merely less than God's (quantitatively); they are in a different class altogether (qualitatively). Freedom is not univocal for sovereigns and dependents: there is a divine freedom and a creaturely freedom. Thus, freedom is ascribed to God and humans *analogically* rather than *univocally*. That is to say, our freedom is an analogy (similar with greater dissimilarities) of God's freedom yet at no point is exactly the same for us both.

2. *Nevertheless, the creature's answering is essential to the making of the covenant.* The covenant is a terrific vista from which to see this relation because, like the creation itself, a treaty involves the decree of a great king and the reply of the servant. Real partnership exists even though the parties are not equal. Apart from the covenantal framework, it is easy to talk about God's sovereignty in almost fatalistic terms, as if the creation is simply an inert puppet that moves only when God specifically decrees it. The creation account, however, actually provides a very different picture. Not only do we read of sovereign fiats ("Let there be . . . !"); we also hear of a certain kind of freedom of the creation to realize its own created destiny ("Let the earth bring forth . . ."). In the same way, God enters into relations with humanity by means of covenants in which there are not only sovereign acts of God, but genuinely free acts of the human partner.

While much of the debate over God's sovereignty and human freedom turns on endless speculation about philosophical possibilities, the covenantal structure of God's relationship to creaturely reality is a much safer and profitable resource. The covenant is always the site where the Great King and his servants are recognized for what they are: unequal partners with their own way of existing, knowing, willing, and acting—one as Creator, the other as creature.

A Nonredemptive Covenant?

After the fall, God might have legitimately disowned his creation but for the eternal and unconditional agreement of the Trinity for the redemption of a people. Both to call out this new people he has chosen and to care even for the rest of humanity hostile to his purposes, God has unconditionally pledged his common grace to all of creation.

The covenant most clearly related to common grace is that which God made with Noah. As we have seen in previous chapters, this covenant is like the one made with Adam and Eve after the fall, the Abrahamic, and the Davidic in that it is unilateral. Despite the fact that they and their descendants will continue to sin, God will fulfill his oath to the very end. Smelling the soothing aroma of the sacrifice Noah offered after leaving the ark, the Lord promised:

> I will never again curse the ground for man's sake, although the imagination of man's heart is evil from his youth; nor will I again destroy every living thing as I have done.
>
> While the earth remains,
> Seedtime and harvest,
> Cold and heat,
> Winter and summer,
> And day and night
> Shall not cease.
> Genesis 8:21–22 NKJV

Just as sin represented an undoing of the righteousness in which humanity was created, the flood represented the undoing of creation itself. This covenant is like a new creation: God swears to uphold creation in its natural processes even in the face of human depravity. It is a covenant that God establishes not only with Noah himself, but "with your descendants after you, and with every living creature that is with you: the birds, the cattle, and every beast of the earth with you, of all that go out of the ark, every beast of the earth. Thus I establish My covenant with you: Never again shall all flesh be cut off by the waters of the flood; never again shall there be a flood to destroy the earth" (9:9–11 NKJV). This covenant has a sacrament also: the rainbow in the sky, as if God were drawing a bow and arrow aimed at himself in heaven should the treaty be violated. It is a peace treaty with the whole creation. We will not find here, however, a promise to redeem sinners or to reconcile them to him through the gift of his Messiah. This is a unilateral oath that does not depend on what humans do, but it is not redemptive. It is a promise to uphold creation in its natural order, not to release it from sin and death.

Although the concept of common grace has been challenged in some circles, it has been generally recognized by Reformed theology as a crucial aspect of biblical teaching. Although the specific term *common grace* is rather recent, the substance is not. Whenever Christians confess their faith in God's benevolent providence toward a world under sin and judgment, we encounter this doctrine.

We see before the Noahic covenant something of a similar sort. If it is not a covenant per se, it is nevertheless in the same vein: what I have in mind here is the mark of Cain (Genesis 4). After the fall, the royal couple is exiled "east of Eden," and heavenly gatekeepers guard the entrance to this earthly paradise that is now surrendered to thorns like a condemned building. Before the fall, the persons and work of Adam and Eve were holy. Even their most mundane daily tasks were part of their mission to extend the kingdom of God throughout all the earth and to confirm all of creation in perfect righteousness. They were to bring their posterity and the whole created order into that Sabbath rest that God himself enjoyed after his six days of labor. Once again we see that humanity was created as an analogy of God at every point. After the fall, however, humanity is by nature no longer holy and cannot by its cultural labors bring about the universal kingdom of God. All of creation, because of Adam, is now under a common curse. Everyone, believer and unbeliever alike, experiences life as painful, difficult, disappointing, and finally, as death. But is that all there is after the fall: a common *curse?*

East of Eden, Adam and Eve build a church, and they also build a state, a civilization, however small its beginnings. No longer is there one covenant with one commission. While the cultural mandate of the creation covenant is still in force ("Be fruitful and multiply," cultivating the earth), it cannot lead to paradise but only to temporal blessing. Now a new covenant has been established that is not based on human performance: it is a unilateral divine promise to send a Messiah who will crush the serpent's head and overturn the curse not only in its temporal, but in its most serious eternal consequences. The sacred and the secular meet in the family of Adam and Eve, as they do in our Christian families today. While our secular vocations are neither saving nor sinful, neither holy nor dishonorable, and we stand shoulder to shoulder with non-Christians in sharing the common blessing of God upon our work, we nevertheless belong to the covenant of grace in which eternal blessings are ours in union with Christ. The family in general is the building block of our secular community, while the Christian family is the building block also of the covenant community. The two cities—the City of Man and the City of God—intersect here. They are not fused together, as in Eden, but they are jointly affirmed. Their common work enjoys God's common blessing despite the common curse, but it will not bring heaven to earth.

This story becomes a bit more complicated with the next generation, however. Even within this covenant home, Abel worships God through the sacrifice God prescribed (foreshadowing Christ), while Cain chooses his own form of worship that is rejected by God. The result is the first religious war: the City of God versus the City of Man. What is truly remarkable is that even after Cain's treason against God and murder of his own brother, God does not wipe him off the face of the earth. Instead of instantly judging Cain, God "marks" him somehow, giving him safe conduct as he is driven away, deeper into exile, as a "fugitive and a vagabond on the earth" (Gen. 4:12 NKJV). "And the Lord said to him, 'Therefore, whoever kills Cain, vengeance shall be taken on him sevenfold'" (v. 15 NKJV).

It is this stay of execution that allows Cain to build a city. In fact, the latter half of this chapter lists the family of Cain as including some of the great pioneers of culture, from the arts to the sciences. Yet it is a proud, cruel, and vengeful city. The chapter closes with a birth announcement: "Adam knew his wife again, and she bore a son and named him Seth, 'For God has appointed another seed for me instead of Abel, whom Cain killed.' And as for Seth, to him also a son was born; and he named him Enosh. Then men began to call on the name of the Lord" (Gen. 4:25–26).

So we begin the story with one creation, one covenant, one people, one mandate, one city. Then after the fall, there is a covenant of creation (with its cultural mandate still in effect for all people, with the law of that covenant universally inscribed on the conscience) and a covenant of grace (with its gospel publicly announced to transgressors), a City of Man (secular but even in its rejection of God, upheld by God's gracious hand for the time being) and a City of God (holy but even in its acceptance by God, sharing in the common curse of a fallen world). Just as the failure to distinguish law covenant from promise covenant leads to manifold confusions in our understanding of salvation, tremendous problems arise when we fail to distinguish adequately between God's general care for the secular order and his special concern for the redemption of his people.

Religious fundamentalism tends to see the world simply divided up into believers and unbelievers. The former are blessed, loved by God, holy, and doers of the right, while the latter are cursed, hated by God, unholy, and doers of evil. Sometimes this is taken to quite an extreme: believers are good people, and their moral, political, and doctrinal causes are always right, always justified, and can never be questioned. Unless the culture is controlled by their agenda, it is simply godless and unworthy of the believers' support.

This perspective ignores the fact that according to Scripture, all of us—believers and unbelievers alike—are simultaneously under a common curse and common grace.

Religious liberalism tends to see the world simply as one blessed community. Ignoring biblical distinctions between those inside and those outside of the covenant community, this approach cannot take the common curse seriously because it cannot take sin seriously. This is a positive, upbeat religion. In truth, no one is under any divine judgment, and everyone enjoys God's richest blessing. Furthermore, this blessing is not only the result of God's *common* grace, but of his *saving* grace. We are not living east of Eden. The holy cause of building the kingdom of God and eliminating all suffering and evil in the world has not been aborted by the fall. Everything is holy.

A biblical doctrine of common grace and covenant will help us to avoid both of these erroneous perspectives. First of all, the human race is not divided at the present time between those who are blessed and those who are cursed. That time is coming, of course, but in this present age, believers and unbelievers alike share in the pains of childbirth, the burdens of labor, the temporal effects of their own sins, and the eventual surrender of their decaying bodies to death. And they also share together in the common blessings of life, such as fruitful wombs and vines, abundant natural resources, marital pleasures, and liberty to realize temporal dreams. Fundamentalists need to learn that salvation and damnation are not the only categories in Scripture. There is in this present age a category for that which is neither holy nor unholy but simply *common*.

Jesus affirmed this third category for this present moment in time: common grace answering to the common curse, in which God sends rain on the just and the unjust alike and calls us to imitate his generosity toward our enemies (Matt. 5:43–48). Jesus also warned his listeners not to impatiently pull up the weeds in God's garden but to wait for his judgment at the end of the age (Matt. 13:24–30). And he rebuked James and John for their bravado in trying to call down fire on the Samaritans who refused to accept their Lord's preaching of the kingdom (Luke 9:51–56).

At the same time, the fact that the human race is not *right now* divided simply between the saved and the lost, the wheat and the tares, should not lead to a cheery but dangerous confidence that this will not happen one day. Even now, Jesus said, those who believe have already passed from death to life, and those who do not believe "stand condemned already" (John 3:15–18 NIV). Furthermore, God's goodness in watering everybody's garden underscores God's kindness in bestowing such temporal goods on people who are not and never will be his friends. In other words, common grace is not saving grace. In fact, unbelievers will use God's patient restraint of his wrath not as an opportunity to embrace his Messiah, but as evidence that there is no judgment in the offing and they can therefore go on in their sins (2 Peter 3:1–9). God does not simply hate unbelievers and leave them to their own devices; he feeds, clothes, heals, and cares for them, and he sends them many earthly pleasures. Yet this does not lead us to conclude that God's love and care for everyone in common grace is the same as his love and care for his elect in saving grace.

Neither the fundamentalist nor the liberal perspective I have characterized here displays much sensitivity to the *historical* aspect of God's dealings. Ironically, both seem to agree that God's relation to unbelievers here and now is a timeless truth: either a sharp judgment between sheep and goats or a benign acceptance of everyone under the banner "God is love." Yet we have seen that the New Testament directs us to greater subtlety. Between the categories of "saved" and "lost" is God's common grace.

What happens "east of Eden" is this: culture is no longer sacred but secular, yet the secular is not literally "godless," a realm beyond God's concern and involvement. Even those who are hostile to the God who has revealed himself in his Word can nevertheless discern right from wrong, for they are created in God's image and the law is written on their consciences, that original charter of their being lingering in their memories like the fragrance of an empty perfume bottle.

Covenant and Eschatology

The last quarter of the nineteenth century witnessed the clash of two eschatologies, or views of history and creation's destiny. One was rooted in the triumphalism that marked Anglo-American Protestantism since the defeat of the Spanish Armada in 1589 and produced the courageous confidence of the New England Puritans. It was eventually secularized in American culture as a generic confidence in our future as God's "redeemer nation" with its own sacred destiny. The other was rooted in the disillusionment that came in the wake of the failure of that dream to materialize in the gradual improvement of society. Most American Protestants before World War I believed that Jesus would return after a golden era of missions and social improvement spreading from the United States to the rest of the world. After "the war to end all wars" didn't, a sea change in eschatological expectations occurred. Now it was easier to believe that Jesus would return before any kind of golden age would even be possible and, in fact, until that return of Christ, things would actually get progressively worse. *Postmillennialism* and *premillennialism* are the terms most commonly used now to delineate those two distinct approaches. *Millennialism* refers to the belief in a literal thousand-year golden age, and *premillennialism* teaches that Jesus must return before the millennium, while *postmillennialism* holds that he will return at the end of it.

So what were most Christians before this postmillennial-premillennial rivalry? These classifications are themselves only about a century old, but the view of most Christians at least since Augustine has been that "the last days" refer to the period between Christ's first and second advents and that we are now living in an age that is marked simultaneously by tribulation and the spread of

God's kingdom through Word and sacrament. In other words, we are living in the period described symbolically in Revelation 20 as a thousand-year reign of Christ, to be followed by Christ's return, when he will hand over the kingdom to his Father. This view is usually called *amillennialism* (i.e., "no-millennialism"), but this is a misnomer, at least for those of us who believe that the millennium is not denied but is in fact a current reality. What we reject is a literalistic interpretation of the thousand years, since the book of Revelation employs numbers symbolically.

Millennialism, whatever the prefix, has a lot to do with the triumph of "Christendom" from the conversion of Constantine the Great to the Great War (World War I). In the fifth century, Augustine sharply distinguished the "two cities," with their own special origin, purpose, destiny, message, and methods. Yet Augustine reluctantly conceded the use of the secular sword in the suppression of the Donatists, a schismatic group not unlike the radical Anabaptists known to the Reformers. Like Augustine, Luther and Calvin defended in theory a "two-kingdoms" approach that they did not always follow in practice. While Augustine, Luther, and Calvin were amillennial in their eschatology, they were still under the sway of the "Christendom" model. Not only can millennialism (whether pre- or post-) become an impetus for identifying some earthly nation, culture, or agenda with the "golden age" of global harmony, but amillennialism was similarly co-opted by secular agendas. By identifying the kingdom of God with the advance of Christianity in the world here and now, it was easy to take the further step of identifying the fortunes of Christianity with those of empire. Christendom is the result of this unholy alliance.

Throughout the Middle Ages, the Holy Roman Empire often played out its identity as the fulfillment of the Old Testament theocracy, the true Israel of God. The emperor was a blend of King David (hence, the *Holy* part of the name) and Caesar (hence, the *Roman* bit). The whole empire and, in fact, all Christian states, composed the *corpus Christianum*, the body of Christ. And this one kingdom of God would grow and spread its unified cult and culture, its worship and its civilization, to the ends of the earth. The body of Christ was not simply a heavenly, spiritual entity made visible in the world through Word, sacrament, discipline, worship, and fellowship in the covenant of grace, but a powerful worldly institution that served the interests of a particular earthly empire.

This is the myth behind the Crusades, the Inquisition, and such American institutions as slavery and the doctrine of "manifest destiny," which gave narrative justification for the slaughter of American Indians. Needless to say, the confusion of the two kingdoms has yielded the lion's share of blame for the atrocities committed in the name of God and his Messiah. In the nineteenth century, most Protestants were optimistic. The emergence of temperance societies was one of many movements organized around the vision of a Christianized America. In the last quarter of that century, fellow evangelicals Josiah Strong and D. L. Moody represented the growing cleavage between the triumphalistic postmillennialists and the pessimistic premillennialists. "The kingdoms of this world will not have become the kingdoms of our Lord," Strong opined, "until the money power has been Christianized."[1] Long before the conservative-liberal polarizations, American evangelicalism had championed the so-called social gospel, as one notices in the following comment from the nineteenth-century evangelical preacher Horace Bushnell, quoted by Strong:

> Talent has been Christianized already on a large scale. The political power of states and kingdoms has been long assumed to be, and now at last really is, as far as it becomes their accepted office to maintain personal security and liberty. Architecture, arts, constitutions, schools, and learning have been largely Christianized. But the money power, which is one of the most operative and grandest of all, is only beginning to be; though with promising tokens of a finally complete reduction to Christ and the uses of His Kingdom. . . . That day, when it comes, is the morning, so to speak, of the new creation. Is it not time for that day to dawn?[2]

But evangelist D. L. Moody marched to the beat of a different drummer. Although Moody was initially quite representative of Charles Finney's social activism, he became increasingly pessimistic about the extent to which earthly empires could become the kingdom of God. "I look upon this world as a wrecked vessel," he would later write. "God has given me a lifeboat and said to me, 'Moody, save all you can.'"[3] Whereas revival was usually regarded as an instrument of Christianizing society through evangelism and social action, Moody saw it as a means of converting individuals: "soul-saving." The American version of the Holy Roman Empire regarded the proliferation of Protestant hospitals, colleges, women's societies, and men's societies as signs of God's approval and, indeed, of the advancement of the kingdom of God.

As George Marsden has documented in various places, both the Christian Right and the Christian Left derive from this late nineteenth-century evangelicalism. It is this quite recent train of thought (or, more precisely, activism), rather than the profound reflection of Augustine and the Reformers, that guides contemporary evangelical activism. Ironically, even staunch premillennialists like Jerry Falwell sound a good deal like the postmillennialists of yesteryear. It is one thing to inconsistently act out a two-kingdoms position and quite another to act out a Christendom model because one has confused a particular culture with the kingdom of God.

We know that Augustine taught the two-kingdoms approach:

These are the two loves: . . . the first is social, the second selfish; the first consults the common welfare for the sake of celestial [heavenly] society, the second grasps at a selfish control of social affairs for the sake of arrogant domination; the first is submissive to God, the second tries to rival God; the first is quiet, the second restless; the first is peaceful, the second, trouble-making; the first prefers truth to the praises of those who are in error, the second is greedy for praise, however it might be obtained. . . . Accordingly, two cities have been formed by two loves: the earthly by the love of self, even to the contempt of God; the heavenly by the love of God, even to the contempt of self.[4]

Accordingly, the earthly kingdoms establish diverse laws and customs that will engender earthly peace—no small accomplishment for humanity after the fall. But the heavenly city is always different in its ambitions, seeking heavenly peace and calling people out of the nations into the kingdom of God. This does not mean that they then are no longer citizens of the earthly city, but that they do not derive their ultimate comfort, satisfaction, or hope from it. Secular society is a gift of God before and after the fall, and it must be cultivated by Christians as well as their non-believing neighbors. In fact, "God can never be believed to have left the kingdoms of men, their dominations and servitudes, outside of the laws of His providence."[5] But the earthly city is always Babylon—it is never converted, as are its inhabitants, into the dwelling place of God. The kingdom of God advances through the proclamation of the gospel, not through force: "This city is therefore now in building; stones are cut down from the hills by the hands of those who preach truth; they are squared that they may enter into an everlasting structure."[6]

Luther appropriated Augustine's New Testament insights, although he reacted against church domination over the secular sphere by making the church subject to the state. (In fairness, the same approach was taken by Zwingli, Bucer, Bullinger, and even to some extent Calvin.)

The two-kingdoms approach represents the Lutheran consensus. But what about Calvin and Calvinism? H. Richard Niebuhr's heavy typecasting in *Christ and Culture* distinguishes Calvinism as a "Christ Transforming Culture" model. That case can be argued. In the Dutch Calvinism of Abraham Kuyper, for instance, we find a heavy emphasis on recognizing the authority of God and of his Christ over all spheres of life and not just religion. While Presbyterianism in the northern United States tended to confuse the two cities, dominated as it came to be by postmillennial optimism, Southern Presbyterianism sharply distinguished the two kingdoms—sometimes perhaps in the interest of protecting the institution of slavery by separating faith from practice.

But when it comes to the confessional standards of Reformed and Presbyterian bodies, as well as their most representative dogmatics or systematic theologies, one easily discerns a consensus around the biblical and Augustinian two-kingdoms doctrine. This should not be surprising: to the extent that one distinguishes the covenant of creation from the covenant of grace, law covenant from promise covenant, Moses and Israel as a theocratic fusion of religion and culture from Abraham and his faith in a heavenly city, one will be likely to distinguish also the kingdom of God from the kingdoms of this world. To demonstrate this conclusion, let's turn briefly to Calvin.

Trained in some of the most distinguished circles of French humanism, Calvin was familiar with a wide range of literature and subjects. Far from repudiating this heritage, he continued to appreciate its strengths even as he came to recognize more clearly the weaknesses in secular thought. "Whenever we come upon these matters in secular writers," he pleads, "let that admirable light of truth shining in them teach us that the mind of man, though fallen and perverted from its wholeness, is nevertheless clothed and ornamented with God's excellent gifts." He continues:

> What then? Shall we deny that the truth shone on the ancient jurists who established civic order and discipline with such great equity? Shall we say that the philosophers were blind in their fine observation and artful description of nature? . . . Shall we say that they are insane who developed medicine, devoting their labor to our benefit? What shall we say of all the mathematical sciences? Shall we consider them the ravings of madmen? . . . Those men whom Scripture calls "natural men" were, indeed, sharp and penetrating in their investigation of earthly things. Let us, accordingly, learn by their example how many gifts the Lord left to human nature even after it was despoiled of its true good.[7]

Opposing what Calvin called the "contrived empire" (i.e., Christendom) was not popular in the sixteenth century, with Roman Catholics or Protestants. And Calvin was still not as clear about how this fell out in practice as we might have hoped. Nevertheless, he insists, we must recognize that we are "under a two-fold government, . . . so that we do not (as commonly happens) unwisely mingle these two, which have a completely different nature." Just as the body and soul are distinct without being necessarily opposed, "Christ's spiritual kingdom and the civil jurisdiction are things completely distinct." But he continues:

> Yet this distinction does not lead us to consider the whole nature of government a thing polluted, which has nothing to do with Christian men. That is what, indeed, certain fanatics who delight in unbridled license shout and boast. . . . But as we have just now pointed out that this kind of government is distinct from that spiritual and inward Kingdom of Christ, so we must know that they are not at variance.[8]

So here the Genevan reformer stood, between the Christ *of* culture (Rome) and the Christ *against* culture (Anabaptists). Recognizing that the world today exhibits neither God's final judgment nor God's final redemption, Calvin embraced this third category: common grace. Because of God's goodness in creation and providence, the secular kingdom could not be renounced without incurring divine displeasure, but because of sin and rebellion against God, the cities of this world would never be reconciled to God apart from his final judgment at the end of history.

Anabaptist zeal to escape the world meets with Calvin's rebuke at every turn. The Schleitheim Confession (1527) of the Anabaptists argued the following dualism that would also heavily mark American fundamentalism:

> We are agreed on separation: A separation shall be made from the evil and from the wickedness which the devil planted in the world; in this manner, simply that we shall not have fellowship

with them [the wicked] and not run with them in the multitude of their abominations. This is the way it is: Since all who do not walk in the obedience of faith, and have not united themselves with God so that they wish to do his will, are a great abomination to God, it is not possible for anything to grow or issue from them except abominable things.[9]

Hence, most Anabaptists withdrew entirely from civil society to form their own communities. Ironically, these communities became a new confusion of kingdoms: the secular and spiritual government were regarded as one and the same, just as they had been in Christendom. While some Anabaptists withdrew, others sought to overthrow existing governments and institute the kingdom of God by force, as in Thomas Muntzer's ill-fated revolution.

The problem with the Anabaptists on this point, Calvin argued, was that they would not distinguish between creation and fall or between the two kingdoms instituted by God. In this way, justification before God was confused with moral, social, and political righteousness, undermining both civility between Christian and non-Christian as well as the gospel. So, Calvin writes, "How malicious and hateful toward public welfare would a man be who is offended by such diversity, which is perfectly adapted to maintain the observance of God's law! For the statement of some, that the law of God given through Moses is dishonored when it is abrogated and new laws preferred to it, is utterly vain."[10] After all, Calvin says, "It is a fact that the law of God which we call the moral law is nothing else than a testimony of natural law and of that conscience which God has engraved on the minds of men."[11] Even unbelievers can rule justly and prudently, as Paul indicates under the more pagan circumstances of his day (Rom. 13:1–7).

Where Calvin differed not only from Luther but from his Reformed elders and colleagues was chiefly in the practice of the two-kingdoms theory. While a nation need not be governed by Christian rulers or Christian laws in order to be just, and Christian conviction does not necessarily demand a certain set of policies, individual believers are simultaneously members of both heavenly and earthly kingdoms and cannot divorce their citizenship in one from the other. One does begin to discern in Reformed attitudes a greater interaction between the two kingdoms. Although both are clearly distinguished, there is perhaps a stronger emphasis in Reformed theology on the continuity of creation and redemption. The image of God is defaced, but not lost, in sinful humanity. While cultural activity can never be redemptive, the redeemed will view creation and cultural activity with new spectacles. The enormous interest in cultural pursuits that the Reformed tradition produced was never seen as entirely separate from heavenly citizenship but part of its embodiment in concern for neighbor.

To be sure, there is a tension in the Reformed position to see all of life under the reign of God and yet to affirm that "we do not yet see all things subjected to Christ." Some err on the side of triumphalism (an over-realized eschatology emphasizing the "already"), while others err on the side of pessimism (an under-realized eschatology emphasizing the "not yet"). But if Calvinists are not expected to endure tyranny, they are also not given liberty to take justice into their own hands or to exercise the judgment reserved for the King of Kings on the last day. Nor are they to seek to impose their distinctively Christian convictions on society through the kingdom of power, as both Rome and the radical Anabaptists tried to do. Rather, they are to pursue their dual citizenship according to the distinct policies proper to each kingdom. The Bible functions as the constitution for the covenant people, not for the secular state.

As I mentioned before, at stake in distinguishing the two kingdoms is the distinction between law and gospel. Those who confuse civil righteousness with righteousness before God will be likely to confuse moral reform in society with the kingdom of God. But here again there is a subtle difference between the Lutheran and Reformed approaches. While the Reformed firmly insist on the distinction and in fact the opposition of law and gospel with respect to the question of our acceptance before God, they do not believe that the law *only* accuses everyone at all times. There is a third use of the law, which Lutherans also accept in principle. According to this use, the law guides believers who can never again fall under its threats and condemnation. Law and gospel are not *in opposition* unless we seek to find satisfaction before God. But they are always *distinguished* at every point. The law can guide us in godly living, but it can never—even after we are justified—give us any life.

Just as we cannot derive any life from the law, we cannot derive any confidence in our cultural triumphs. As with law and gospel, our earthly and heavenly citizenship are not opposed unless we are seeking a way of salvation for a nation. But once we recognize that there is no everlasting rest from violence, oppression, injustice, and immorality through our own political or cultural works, we are free to pursue their amelioration with vigorous gratitude to God for his saving grace in Jesus Christ. Furthermore, we pursue this cultural task looking back to the creation, which God blessed, and looking forward to this same creation, which will be restored when the kingdoms of this world will finally be made the kingdom of our God and of his Christ forever, world without end.

7

The Covenant People

GIVEN ALL THAT we have learned thus far, the obvious question remains: What are the continuity and discontinuity between the old and new covenants—which is also to say, between Israel and the church? Does Scripture itself yield a covenantal interpretation of the nature of the church? If so, what difference does it make to the practical life of believers in community and communion together with their covenant Lord?

One People or Two?

Dispensational premillennialism, generally associated with a certain type of conservative Protestantism, despite recent revisions, considers the distinction between Israel and the church axiomatic. While many of its representatives have moved away from an extreme position that commits old covenant Israelites to salvation by works in contrast to salvation by grace in the new covenant, this strong discontinuity between two distinctive covenants and peoples in God's plan remains firmly in place.[1] Mainline Protestant scholars increasingly argue that God has two distinct plans for Israel and the church.[2] Although operating within widely divergent theologies, this principle of sharply distinguishing Israel and the church, allowing to each its own covenant with God, would appear to be a majority position within contemporary Protestantism.

Both dispensationalists and mainline theologians often employ a similar critique of traditional Christian teaching, which they often refer to by the labels "replacement theology" or "supercessionism" (i.e., the church's having superseded or replaced the nation of Israel in God's plan).

Without focusing on the rival views and their criticisms of supercessionism, my goal in this chapter is to lay out a covenantal position that, I hope, avoids the extremes of both replacement theology and the notion of two peoples with two distinct plans of salvation.

So far I have tried to point out that from the beginning Israel knew of two distinct covenants. The Sinai covenant, in which the people swore to "do everything written in the Law," required absolute, total obedience: to disobey at one point was to be guilty of violating the whole pact. The promise was conditional: if you do everything I command, you will live long in the land I am giving you. To be sure, the land grant itself was based on God's gracious deliverance of the people from Egypt, but it was now theirs to lose or keep depending on how well they did in their probation in the land. In this respect, the Sinai covenant was a covenant of works, a reiteration of the covenant between God and humanity in Adam. Yet there was also a covenant of pure promise, a unilateral covenant of peace that God had sworn to Abraham, Isaac, and Jacob. Unlike a suzerainty treaty, it was unconditional and in form corresponded to the Noahic covenant. In both form and content it corresponded to the "everlasting" Davidic covenant, leading on to the new covenant in Jeremiah 31 and elsewhere.

In this light, there is some reason to say that there is a distinction between Israel and the church. However—and this is where the covenantal view expounded here differs sharply from those above—it is not a distinction between the Old Testament and the New, as if they provided for two different ways of salvation or communion with God. Rather, it is a distinction *within* both testaments, arising from two different covenants: a national covenant that Israel made with God at Sinai and a gracious covenant that God makes with believers and their children. The covenant of law pertains to the nation's remaining in the earthly land; the covenant of promise pertains to the eternal inheritance in Jesus Christ, Abraham's seed. No *Israelite* was ever justified by works, but the *nation* had to keep the conditions of the law in order to remain in possession of the earthly type of the heavenly rest. The prophets, culminating in John the Baptist and Jesus, brought the ax to the root of the tree: the earthly Jerusalem is now in bondage with her children. Only in Christ can anyone, Jew or Gentile, be a child of Abraham.

Is God Through with Israel?

This view challenges both supercessionism and the "two peoples" theology of recent discussions. It challenges the former because, instead of seeing the church as Israel's replacement, it regards it as Israel's fruition. Paul labors in Romans 9–11 to make several points along this line, under the general heading that God has not failed in his promises to Israel. First, he says that all along God has exercised his sovereign prerogative to elect whom he will and to pass over others, even within Israel (e.g., Isaac and Ishmael, Jacob and Esau). Second, he says that God temporarily blinded Israel so that Gentiles may be incorporated into the covenant of grace. Third, he tells us that this blinding is neither complete (citing himself as evidence that even now God is calling Jews to the Messiah) nor final (appealing to a large-scale conversion of his fellow Jews at the end of the age). Gentile believers are not to become haughty in their covenantal identity (as supercessionism encourages), since they are only grafted onto the holy vine of

Israel. Although woefully brief, this summarizes the entire thrust of Paul's mission to the Gentiles and his view of the relation between Israel and the church. The church does not replace Israel. Recalling the fig tree that withered at Jesus's curse, symbolizing the pronouncement of woes and the parables of the kingdom, the picture is of an Israel that, despite its *national* judgment as a covenant-breaker, is nevertheless kept alive by extensive pruning and grafting at the level of *individual* salvation through Christ. After bringing in the full number of elect Gentiles, God will pour out his Spirit on the Jewish people en masse (Rom. 11:25–32).

Covenant and Canon

We have already seen in chapter 1 how closely the Hebrew Scriptures (particularly the Torah) parallel ancient Near Eastern treaties. This is true not only in content (historical prologue, stipulations, sanctions), but in ceremonial form as well: the identification of the treaty tablets with the treaty itself, the solemn cutting rituals of self-malediction for violation of the treaty, and the placement of the tablets in the shrines of each party, calling the gods and nature to witness to its decrees.

These clear parallels with ancient treaties may be found in sections of the Pentateuch that form the most concentrated material constituting the Sinaitic canon (Exod. 25:16, 21; 40:20; Deut. 4:2; 10:2; 31:9–13; cf. Deuteronomy 27; Josh. 8:30–35).

While the basic structure of the treaties could not be emended, various renewals would occur, taking into account historical changes as well as continuity. Kline writes:

> The legal compatibility of these two aspects, the eternal and the changing, must have resided in a recognition of a distinction between the fundamental tributary allegiance of the vassal to the great king (or the peaceful mutual stance of the partners to a parity treaty), which was theoretically and ideally permanent,

and the precise details, such as boundary definitions and tribute specifications, etc, which were subject to alteration.[3]

Such covenants are made between unequal partners, and they cannot be emended by secretaries. New covenants may be drawn up but are never corrected.[4] Extant ancient Near Eastern documents of this treaty type, a form that became widely used in international diplomacy by the time of Moses, consistently demonstrate this impossibility of emendation or alteration on the part of the vassal. For instance, one such treaty declares, "Whoever . . . changes but one word of this tablet . . . may the thousand gods of this tablet root that man's descendants out of the land of Hatti."[5] This form is followed in the Deuteronomic form of the biblical covenant: "You shall not add to the word which I command you, nor take from it, that you may keep the commandments of the LORD your God which I command you" (Deut. 4:2 NKJV). The same covenantal judgment is found in John's apocalypse: "I warn everyone who hears the words of the prophecy of this book: if anyone adds to them, God will add to that person the plagues described in this book; if anyone takes away from the words of the book of this prophecy, God will take away that person's share in the tree of life and in the holy city, which are described in this book" (Rev. 22:18–19 NRSV). In fact, chapters 2–3 reflect the covenant lawsuit pattern of the Prophets.

"In a manner analogous to other ancient treaties, the Old Testament as canonical covenant was both 'forever' and yet subject to change"—changes determined by the Covenant Maker's purposes in redemptive history.[6] Thus, God's "unchangeable oath" and "everlasting covenant" in election and redemption can be administered in history through all the variety and contingencies that the biblical traditions themselves evidence.

It follows from the covenantal character of Old and New Testament canonicity, at once "forever" and yet subject to revision, that Scripture is not a closed canon in some general, absolute sense.

In fact, instead of speaking of the canon of Scripture it were better to speak of the Old and New Testament canons, or of the canonical covenants which constitute the Scripture. Each authoritative covenantal corpus is of fixed extent, but the historical order of which it is constitutional is not a perpetually closed system. The Old and New Testaments are discrete covenantal canons in series. Each is of divine authority in all its parts, but that does not imply the absolutizing of its norms in abstraction from the covenantally structured historical process. . . . Each inscripturated covenant is closed to vassal's alteration, subtraction, or addition (as the proscriptions of the treaty document clauses insist), yet each is open to revision by the Suzerain, revision that does not destroy but fulfills, as the history of God's kingdom proceeds from one epochal stage to the next, particularly, in the passage from the old covenant to the new. "Closed" as a general description of a canon would be suitable only in the eternal state of the consummation. Another corollary of covenantal canonicity is that the Old Testament is not the canon of the Christian church. From a strictly legal standpoint, the Old Testament viewed in its identity as the historical treaty by which God ordered the life of pre-messianic Israel belongs to the church's historical archives rather than to its constitution. Covenant Theology is completely Biblical in its insistence on the Christological unity of the Covenant of Redemption as both law and gospel in its old and new administrations; nevertheless, the old covenant is not the new covenant.[7]

Canon and covenant are mutually determinative.

Written to dissuade converted Jews from returning to Judaism during the persecution targeting Christians, the Epistle to the Hebrews is pregnant with contrasts between the earthly (old covenant) and the heavenly (new covenant), a pattern that we will pick up on in a later chapter. There is a temporary, transitory, even now vanishing aspect of the old economy as it yields to the new covenant and its better promises, mediator, priesthood, temple, sacrifice, and homeland. "What is riding on Israel's obedience to the covenant in Deuteronomy," says Steven McKenzie, "is nothing less than its status as God's chosen people and its survival in the promised land."[8] To be sure, the original bequest of the land was a gift, but Israel must keep it by faithfulness. To borrow from E. P. Sanders's famous definition of covenantal nomism, they got in by grace but stayed in by obedience. McKenzie adds, "Disobedience would result in the loss of the land and the expulsion of the people (8:19–20; 11:16–17). The ceremony on Mounts Ebal and Gerizim described near the end of Deuteronomy (27–28) lays out the alternatives: blessings for obedience, unspeakable curses for disobedience."[9] How different from such covenantal nomism is the expectation that comes from the new covenant, in fulfillment of the royal promises of the Abrahamic and Davidic covenants: "For you have not come to the mountain that may be touched . . ." (Heb. 12:18 NKJV). And because of this, all the nations stream not to Sinai but to Zion for their part in the new creation, in the great parade of the creature kingdoms before their Creator in the everlasting Sabbath day.

8

Signs and Seals of the Covenant

A s t h e   S p i r i t   of Promise, the Third Person of the Trinity brings to fruition Christ's "new creation." The Father speaks, the Son is spoken, and the Spirit brings about in history the effect and perfection of that speech. But how does the Spirit accomplish this? According to Scripture, it is by the gift of faith. But where does this faith come from? It is created by the preaching of the gospel and confirmed by the sacraments as signs and seals of God's covenant promises.

Treaty ceremonies in our day are different from those of the Old Testament. Many of us recall the stunning photograph of Anwar Sadat and Menachem Begin signing the peace treaty between Egypt and Israel or other treaty signings where the parties embraced. State dinners are often held to consummate a treaty. In more mundane agreements, we shake hands on a deal.

The ceremonies of the sacraments belong to this world of covenant-making. Every time we witness a baptism or receive Communion, God is shaking hands on the deal he has made with us. To be sure, there are two parties—we are shaking hands as well—but in this covenant his are the hands that enfold ours.

137

While we must believe the promises given in the covenant, God is the guarantor of the treaty.

> The saying is sure:
> If we have died with him, we will also live with him;
> if we endure, we will also reign with him;
> if we deny him, he will also deny us;
> if we are faithless, he remains faithful—for he cannot deny himself.
>
> 2 Timothy 2:11–13 NRSV

Both the Old and New Testaments confirm this identity of the sacraments as "signs and seals," which is clearly the language of covenant ratification. As we have already seen, making a covenant is seen as *cutting* a covenant: the ratification ceremony is inextricable from the covenant itself. At Sinai, says Vos, the idea of covenant is found "entirely in the ceremony of ratification."[1] How can this enrich our understanding of and appreciation for these great benefits?

God's Presence as Treaty (Word) and Ratification (Sacrament)

James Hastings writes in the *Encyclopedia of Religion and Ethics* of "the great distinction between Christian and all other forms of worship."

> The object elsewhere is to produce some theurgic effect. The idea is to operate upon the Deity through sacrifice and prayer, and by defective symbolism to attain to some connection, some union, with the god. This is the case in the heathen world generally, and also in the temple worship of Judaism. Only in the Synagogue and in the Christian forms of service is the central place given to God's word, as it speaks to [the]assembled congregation out of the sacred book with voice of instruction, edification, and exhortation.[2]

While Hastings erroneously sweeps the temple worship of the old covenant into the characterization of "defective symbolism" attempting to manipulate the Deity, he is basically correct in observing the sharp contrast between biblical religion and its rivals. Even in some forms of Christianity, the impression is often given (and backed up with theological fine print) that God can be placated by our sacrifices and manipulated to do our bidding with sufficiently pious and liturgical incantations. In biblical faith, however, the point is to be summoned and addressed by and bound to the covenant Lord. It is no wonder that the Word takes pride of place.

> They heard the sound [*qol*, "voice"] of the LORD God walking in the garden in the cool of the day, and the man and his wife hid themselves from the presence [*panim*, "face"] of the LORD God among the trees of the garden. But the LORD God called to the man and said to him, "Where are you?" And he said, "I heard the sound [*qol*, "voice"] of you in the garden, and I was afraid, because I was naked, and I hid myself."
>
> Genesis 3:8–10

This was the first but certainly not the last time that God's presence would come as bad news as well as good. For those who are rightly related to him, God's presence is a blessing. To place oneself in God's hands of salvation and protection is to find security. Otherwise, "It is a fearful thing to fall into the hands of the living God" (Heb. 10:31 NKJV).

God is everywhere—omnipresent. Therefore, when we talk about God being "near" or "far off," we are speaking of our relationship with him. As the Reformers saw so clearly, the question about God's presence is not abstract, as implied in the philosophical query we begin asking as children: "Mommy, where is God?" The question, rather, is very concrete, especially since our problem is concrete: *Where is God for me, for us, given where we are (in sin and death)?* Before the fall, Adam and Eve delighted in God's nearness; afterward, they feared the sound of his footsteps.

Whenever Israel wanted to presume on God's gracious nearness while disregarding his will, the result was idolatry: at last, a god who could be near without instilling fear and an ominous threat of judgment for violation. We recognize the striking contrast between the demeanor of the Israelites when God addressed them in speech and when they fabricated an image of Yahweh. In the former case, they were filled with terror (Exod. 20:18–21). They stood at a distance and cried out for Moses's mediation. As the writer to the Hebrews informs us, this was "a voice whose words made the hearers beg that no further messages be spoken to them. For they could not endure the order that was given" (Heb. 12:19–20). But in the presence of the golden calf, "the people sat down to eat and drink and rose up to play" (Exod. 32:6).

In the wake of the golden calf episode and the patriarch's effective intercession on behalf of the people to keep God from destroying them, Moses argues his case for God's presence—that is, his own *shekinah* glory, to accompany, defend, and lead Israel:

> Moses said to the LORD, "See, you say to me, 'Bring up this people,' but you have not let me know whom you will send with me. Yet you have said, 'I know you by name, and you have also found favor in my sight.' Now therefore, if I have found favor in your sight, please show me now your ways, that I may know you in order to find favor in your sight. Consider too that this nation is your people." And he said, "My presence will go with you, and I will give you rest." And he said to him, "If your presence will not go with me, do not bring us up from here. For how shall it be known that I have found favor in your sight, I and your people? Is it not in your going with us, so that we are distinct, I and your people, from every other people on the face of the earth?"
>
> And the LORD said to Moses, "This very thing that you have spoken I will do, for you have found favor in my sight, and I know you by name." Moses said, "Please show me your glory." And he said, "I will make all my goodness pass before you and will proclaim before you my name 'The LORD.' And I will be gracious to whom I will be gracious, and will show mercy on whom I will show

mercy. But," he said, "you cannot see my face, for man shall not
see me and live." And the Lord said, "Behold, there is a place by
me where you shall stand on the rock, and while my glory passes
by I will put you in a cleft of the rock, and I will cover you with
my hand until I have passed by. Then I will take away my hand,
and you shall see my back, but my face shall not be seen."

Exodus 33:12–23

Several things are obvious on the surface: first, that Yahweh's
answer—that is, his presence—is in response to Moses's need
for reassurance of his calling and that of the people whom he has
redeemed. More specifically still, it answers Moses's request for
confirmation that he has indeed found favor in God's sight and
will continue to do so. This is not only for him: "Consider too that
this nation is your people" (v. 13). Yahweh's answer, "My presence
[*panim*, "face"] will go with you, and I will give you rest" (v. 14),
reaffirms his covenant oath to Abraham, Isaac, and Jacob. Moses's
and Israel's election and set-apartness is hollow apart from this
presence: "For how shall it be known that I have found favor in
your sight, I and your people?" (v. 16a). It is not their righteousness but Yahweh's presence that is identified as the distinguishing
mark between Israel and the nations (v. 16b).

After Yahweh reaffirms his promised presence, Moses takes
advantage of the opportunity to gain greater intimacy with his
covenant Lord. What stands out in this second half of the pericope
is the impossibility of seeing God's face—yet God's voluntary condescension in revealing himself in a manner that is safe for human
beings. This revelation, which is the form that God's making his
presence known to Moses takes, is an announcement—a sermon,
as it were. God will not display his majestic glory (his face, *panim* in
the sense of full presence), but only his back. Moses's seeing God's
back, while being sheltered from the radiation of God's *shekinah*,
actually amounts to him hearing God's goodness proclaimed. To
see God as he is in all of his glory—*deus nudus*—is what Moses
requests, but it is the accommodated revelation of God's good-

ness and grace that is in Moses's (and the people's) best interest because God's full presence is overwhelming to finite creatures and terrifying to the consciences of sinful creatures. Yahweh will signify his presence by means of words, theophanic glory cloud, ark of the covenant, tabernacle, and eventually temple, but he will never manifest his face (full presence) to creatures in their present frame.

The Aaronic blessing, "The LORD make his face to shine upon you" (Num. 6:25), is equivalent to the phrases in which it is nestled: "The LORD bless you and keep you" (v. 24) and "the LORD lift up his countenance [*panim*] upon you and give you peace" (v. 26). "So shall they [the priests] put my name upon the people of Israel, and I will bless them" (v. 27). The request for the revelation of God's goodness meets the same answer in Psalm 4:6: "There are many who say, 'Who will show us some good? Lift up the light of your face upon us, O LORD!'" God's face is God's presence, and this presence is understood by the Israelites as an index of his favor toward them. This is further demonstrated in the fact that when God's "countenance" or "face" is not "lifted up" or "enlightened," fear fills the people: "The face of the LORD is against those who do evil, to cut off the memory of them from the earth." On the other hand, "The LORD is near to the brokenhearted and saves the crushed in spirit" (Ps. 34:16, 18; repeated in 1 Peter 3:10–12). Notice again the close connection between God's *face* and God's *nearness* in compassion.

Even in the Messiah, who is "the image of the invisible God," creator of all things, in whom "all the fullness of God was pleased to dwell" (Col. 1:15–19), the full presence of God in his blinding glory is deferred. For now, it is enough that the incarnate Son has revealed God's "back"—his condescension in grace, as Colossians goes on to relate:

> For in him all the fullness of God was pleased to dwell, and through him to reconcile to himself all things, whether on earth or in heaven, making peace by the blood of his cross.

And you, who once were alienated and hostile in mind, doing evil deeds, he has now reconciled in his body of flesh by his death, in order to present you holy and blameless and above reproach before him.

verses 19–22

In fact, this is Paul's ministry: "to make the *word* of God fully known, the mystery hidden for ages and generations but now revealed to his saints," which is "Christ in you, the hope of glory. Him we *proclaim*" (vv. 25–28, emphasis added). Paul in Romans 10 also argues that in the logic of divine descent (condescension), which is identified with "the righteousness based on faith" opposed to "the righteousness that is based on the law," the presence of God in this semi-eschatological age is as near as "the word of faith that we proclaim." One need not climb into heaven or descend into the depths (Rom. 10:5–8). "For 'everyone who calls on the name of the Lord will be saved'" (v. 13). The presence of God is to be sought in his Word, and God's gracious presence is to be sought more particularly in "the word of faith." "So faith comes from hearing, and hearing through the word of Christ" (v. 17).

Repeatedly we encounter this emphasis on the word that is heard corresponding to the order of promise in a covenant of grace, in contrast to a vision that is seen corresponding to an order of consummation. "Now we see through a glass, darkly; but then face to face" (1 Cor. 13:12 KJV). Even now, in the face of Christ, we participate eschatologically in the glory to come. "For God, who said, 'Let light shine out of darkness,' has shone in our hearts to give the light of the knowledge of the glory of God in the face of Jesus Christ" (2 Cor. 4:6). Yet this still does not escape the order of promise—the word of the gospel, the proclamation concerning Christ, the mystery now revealed, the light of the knowledge of God in Christ. Only in the consummation is the full presence of God seen, and that in the face of the glorified Son: "In his right hand he held seven stars, from his mouth came a sharp two-edged sword, and his face was like the sun shining in full strength" (Rev. 1:16).

At the tree of life, fed by the river of life, "No longer will there be anything accursed, but the throne of God and of the Lamb will be in it, and his servants will worship him. They will see his face, and his name will be on their foreheads" (Rev. 22:3–4).

All of these terms we have encountered above: the name (calling on the name, being given the name), word, proclamation, promise, presence, the divine witnessing involved in God's countenance, and so on, are part of the vocabulary of covenant rather than metaphysics. They belong to history rather than eternal forms and are drawn analogically from the world of ancient Near Eastern international diplomacy. In the Word of command and promise, we discover who we are: the law tells us that we are "under sin" by nature; the gospel tells us that we are "in Christ" through faith. This is the Word of the Covenant, but in both Old and New Testaments we learn also of the signs and seals of the covenant that ratify the treaty of peace.

Cutting a Covenant: Circumcision and Baptism

Especially since the Old and New Testaments both describe circumcision/baptism and Passover/the Lord's Supper as signs and seals of the covenant, we will briefly consider the relation of covenant and sacrament. First, in Genesis 15, God's covenant with Abram is inaugurated with what may appear to us at first as only an odd ritual. Prior to the ritual itself, God had proclaimed his covenant oath: a decidedly one-sided promise. Despite the fact that Genesis 15 is a narrative of the covenant-making rather than the covenant itself, the formal structure is still present.

Clearly the goal of the cutting ritual about to be enacted is to confirm Abram's doubts about Yahweh's spoken promise. "To his promise to Abraham God added a second immutable thing (Heb. 6:17, 18)," Kline notes.[3] Even after showing Abram the stars to indicate the innumerable heirs who will come from Sarah's barren womb, the patriarch's faith still wavers: "O Lord GOD, how am I to know that I shall possess it?" (Gen. 15:8 NRSV). Then God commands the odd ritual: animals are "cut in half," either half placed on opposite sides of what would appear to be an aisle. Abram did as God told him, and God confirmed his oath with the vision of the divine Promise Keeper walking through the halves. As we have already seen, this ritual would have been well known in the ancient Near East, although its one-sidedness distinguishes it from typical suzerainty treaties in which the vassal would be made to take upon himself the oath and its terrible curses for violation. As in a well-known secular treaty of Ashurnirari, king of Assyria, the slaughtered ram is set apart from its ordinary function in order to represent the vassal and his people:

> This ram is not brought from his herd for sacrifice, nor is he brought out for a *garitu*-festival, nor is he brought out for a *kinitu*-festival, nor is he brought out for (a rite for) a sick man, nor is he brought out for slaughter a[s. . . .] It is to make the treaty of Ashurnirari, King of Assyria, with Mati'ilu that he is brought out. If Mati'ilu [sins] against the treaty sworn by the gods, just as this ram is broug[ht here] from his herd and to his herd will not return [and stand] at its head, so may Mati'ilu with his sons, [his nobles,] the people of his land [be brought] far from his land and to his land not return [to stand] at the head of his land. This head is not the head of a ram; it is the head of Mati'ilu, the head of his sons, his nobles, the people of his land. If those named [sin] against this treaty, as the head of this ram is c[ut] off, his leg put in his mouth [. . .] so may the head of those named be cut off[. . . .] This shoulder is not the shoulder of a ram, it is the shoulder of the one named, it is the shoulder of [his sons, his nobles], the people of his land. If Mati'ilu sins against this treaty, as the shou[lder of this ram] is torn out, [. . .] so may the [shoulder of the one na]med, [his] sons, [his nobles,] the people of [his land] be torn out [. . .] (Col. 1:10ff.).[4]

In Abram's vision, Yahweh himself takes a solitary self-maledictory oath, calling down upon his own head the curses of the law that he himself has imposed in the case even of the human partner's malfeasance.

Understandably, to *make* a covenant was to *cut* a covenant (*karat berit*). So close was the representative identification of the forswearer with the ritual animal and the sign with the thing signified that circumcision was called simply "the covenant." Zipporah, Moses's Midianite wife, expressed her astonishment as to the "bloody" character of the religion of Yahweh (specifically in reference to circumcision; Exod. 4:25–26).

Covenant and blood are inextricably linked in biblical faith. As O. Palmer Robertson notes, "A covenant is a bond in blood sovereignly administered."[5] *Berit* is frequently used together with the verb *karat* ("cut"), so that making a covenant is a matter of cutting a covenant. "This phrase 'to cut a covenant' does not appear just at one stage in the history of the biblical covenants. Much to the contrary, it occurs prominently across the entire spread of the Old Testament. The law, the prophets, and the writings all contain the phrase repeatedly."[6] Hence, a covenant is a "pledge to the death."

> This interpretation finds strong support in the words of the prophet Jeremiah. As he recalls Israel's disloyalty to their covenant commitments, he reminds them of the ritual by which they "passed between the parts of the calf" (Jer. 34:18). By their transgression, they have called down on themselves the curses of the covenant. Therefore they may expect dismemberment of their own bodies. Their carcasses "shall be food for the birds of the sky and the beasts of the earth" (Jer. 34:20). . . . The phrase "bond in blood" accords ideally with the biblical emphasis that "apart from shedding of blood there is no remission" (Heb. 9:22). . . . The life is in the blood (Lev. 17:11) and so the shedding of blood represents a judgment on life.[7]

In Genesis 17, the covenant with Abraham and his seed was "cut" quite literally by the rite of circumcision. In other words, circumcision ratified the covenant, put it into force with respect to the one presented for it.

"Cutting off" is throughout the Old Testament (and the New) the synonym for being rejected by God. Kline shows that while Isaac's circumcision in Genesis 17 is merely a symbolic "cutting off," indicating his passing through the blood ordeal of divine judgment to belong to God's people, the offering up of Isaac's entire person as a burnt offering in chapter 22 is different. "In the circumcision of the foreskin on the eighth day he had passed under the judgment knife of God apart from God's altar in a merely symbolic, token act of conditional malediction. But this cutting off of the whole body of Isaac's flesh to be consumed in the fire of the altar of God was a falling under the actual judgment curse."[8] Of course, the angel from Yahweh aborted the sacrifice of Isaac by providing a ram caught in the thicket.

This controversial episode of the so-called sacrifice of Isaac had already been anticipated in the smoking firepot theophany in chapter 15, "the Old Testament Golgotha."[9] Just as God placed himself under the self-maledictory curse in chapter 15, symbolized by the smoking firepot walking through the severed animals, so here in chapter 22 he takes Isaac's place symbolically by the ram caught in the thicket. He will come under his own knife. No wonder Paul called the cross "the circumcision of Christ" (Col. 2:11). Kline reminds us that, like Isaac, Jesus was circumcised as an infant, "that partial and symbolic cutting off" in the moment prophetically chosen to name him Jesus.

> But it was the circumcision of Christ in crucifixion that answered to the burnt-offering of Genesis 22 as a perfecting of circumcision, a "putting off" not merely of a token part but "of the [whole] body of the flesh" (Col. 2:11, ARV), not simply a symbolic oath-cursing but a cutting off of "the body of his flesh through death" (Col. 1:22) in accursed darkness and dereliction.[10]

It was Jesus of whom Isaiah prophesied:

All we like sheep have gone astray;
  we have turned every one to his own way;
and the LORD has *laid on him*
  the iniquity of us all. . . .
By oppression and judgment he *was taken away*;
  and as for his generation, who considered
that he was *cut off* out of the land of the living,
  stricken for the transgression of my people?
And they made his grave with the wicked
  and with a rich man in his death,
although he had done no violence,
  and there was no deceit in his mouth.
Yet it was the will of the LORD to crush him;
  he has put him to grief;
when his soul makes *an offering for sin*,
  he shall see his offspring; he shall prolong his days;
the will of the LORD shall prosper in his hand. . . .
yet he bore the sin of many,
  and makes intercession for the transgressors.

Isaiah 53:6–12

United to Christ in his circumcision-death, the baptized too come under God's sword of judgment. "It is a judicial death as the penalty for sin," says Kline. "Yet to be united with Christ in his death is also to be raised with him whom death could not hold in his resurrection unto justification."[11] He bears the sanctions, the curse ("cutting off") and the blessing (justification and life); and we participate in this union through faith. Ultimately, Jesus's actions are an eschatological sign of judgment and justification. "Here Old Testament prophecy proclaims the New Testament's deliverance out of the malediction of human circumcision by pointing to the malediction-benediction of the circumcision-resurrection of Christ."[12]

John's baptism "is emphatically a sign of eschatological judgment," a covenant lawsuit—an ultimatum in the spirit of the prophets.[13] "The axe was even now 'laid unto the root' to inflict this judgment of circumcision (cf. Matt. 3:7ff.; Luke 3:7ff.)."[14] The two dominant forms of trial for determining whether one had committed a crime were water ordeals and fire ordeals. John the Baptist invoked these trials by saying that the one to come after him would baptize with the Spirit and with fire (Matt. 3:11). Similarly, Peter compared baptism to the flood through which Noah and his family safely passed, while warning of the future judgment by fire for unbelievers (2 Peter 3:5–7). While the Pharisees were also baptizing followers as a purification rite, John's baptism was decidedly different: it invoked the eschatological judgment. It was a sign and seal of the judgment, a trial by ordeal.

> The time had come when here in the Jordan River, where once Yahweh had declared through an ordeal that the promised land belonged to Israel, he was requiring the Israelites to confess their forfeiture of the blessing of his kingdom and their liability to the wrath to come. Yet John's proclamation was a preaching of "good tidings" to the people (Lk. 3:18) because it invited the repentant to anticipate the messianic judgment in a symbolic ordeal in the Jordan, so securing for themselves beforehand a verdict of remission of sin against the coming judgment.[15]

Likewise, "Paul described Israel's Red Sea ordeal as being baptized (1 Cor. 10:2), and Peter in effect calls the Noahic deluge ordeal a baptism (1 Peter 3:21)." So too the Baptist declares, "He shall baptize you with the Holy Spirit and with fire" (Matt. 3:11f.; Luke 3:16f.; cf. Mark 1:8).[16]

> John called attention to the great difference; his own baptism was only a symbol, whereas the coming One would baptize men in an actual ordeal with the very elements of divine power.... By his baptism Jesus was consecrating himself unto his sacrificial death in the judicial ordeal of the cross...: "I have a baptism to be baptized with" (Luke 12:50; cf. Mark 10:38).[17]

Jesus's appeal to the sign of Jonah recalls the ancient association of Satan with the dragon. And as Jesus goes down into the Jordan, he is already wrestling with the dragon-fish in anticipation of the cross and resurrection.[18] "We cannot, therefore, but view with new appreciation the liturgies of the ancient church when they speak of Jesus crushing the head of the dragon in his descent into the river for baptism."[19] John's baptism was a renewal of circumcision, while Jesus brought believers into the reality of the new covenant.

Jesus begins his ministry in the "ultimatum" stage created by the covenant lawsuit brought by John. In fact, says Kline, John's imprisonment "was the signal for the departure of Jesus to Galilee," with the announcement "that now the time was fulfilled and the kingdom at hand (Matt. 4:17; Mark 1:15), and with its heralding, in the Nazareth synagogue, of the arrival of the acceptable year of the Lord (Luke 4:19, 21)."[20]

Jesus's baptism is an ordeal, like the flood (1 Peter 3:20–22). In this passage, since "a saving function is predicated of the waters of baptism (v. 21), the waters should also figure as a means of salvation in the deluge episode (v. 20)." Noah and his family were saved by this "baptism" in that their having safely passed through the trial by water testified and in fact certified to them and to all ages that they had been vindicated. This baptism, says Peter, is not a mere washing off of bodily filth, but a cleansing of the conscience. "Now conscience has to do with accusing and excusing; it is forensic. Baptism, then, is concerned with man in the presence of God's judgment throne."[21]

Here, as in the exodus, we are reminded by the prophet of the eschatological nature of both the water and fire ordeals:

> But now thus says the LORD,
> he who created you, O Jacob,
>   he who formed you, O Israel:
> "Fear not, for I have redeemed you;
>   I have called you by name, you are mine.

> When you pass through the waters, I will be with you;
>   and through the rivers, they shall not overwhelm you;
> when you walk through the fire, you shall not be burned,
>   and the flame shall not consume you.
> For I am the Lord your God,
>   the Holy One of Israel, your Savior."
>
>   Isaiah 43:1–3

If Peter relates baptism to the deliverance through water, Paul relates it to a new exodus in 1 Corinthians 10. Here we see that the fire theophany as the pillar of fire which also appeared to Moses in the burning bush is judicial. "In the exodus crisis the pillar served to shelter, guide, and protect the elect nation; it thereby rendered for Israel a favorable verdict (cf. Exod. 13:21f.; 14:19f.)" but was a fire of condemnation for the Egyptians.[22] This fiery pillar "is a defense and glory" for Israel (Isa. 4:2–5).[23]

In neither case, baptism "into Moses" or "into Christ," is the question about cleansing. It belongs to the realm of the law court; it is judicial:

> What the apostle meant when he said that the fathers were bap-
> tized into Moses in their passage under the cloud and through
> the sea was that the Lord thereby brought them into an ordeal
> by those elements, an ordeal through which he declared them
> accepted as the servant people of his covenant and so under the
> authority of Moses, his mediatorial viceregent.[24]

In the same way, after his baptism into death, Christ "was raised for our justification" (Rom. 4:25). The newness of the new covenant, then, is not the abolition of the law but its fulfillment finally through a substitute, a representative head.[25] It is not true that the old covenant had both threats and promises and the new covenant has only promises, for Christ still "stands like the theophanic ordeal pillar of fire in the midst of the seven churches," in threat and promise, and warns through his apostle that Gentiles grafted onto the covenantal tree can be broken off (Rom. 11:17–21; cf. Matt. 8:12; John 15:1–8; Heb. 6:4–8).[26]

So then, baptism is even more pregnant with import than was circumcision under the old covenant, for it is the sacrament of a greater reality in which God's judgment and justification are present now in Christ by his Spirit. "Christian baptism is a sign of the eschatological ordeal in which the Lord of the covenant brings his servants to account": justification and life for those who are united to him by faith; condemnation and death for those who remain "in Adam"—even if they have been formally related to the covenant people. Those who reject the promises ratified by this ritual are in the position of those in the wilderness generation: "For good news came to us just as to them, but the message they heard did not benefit them, because they were not united by faith with those who listened" (Heb. 4:2).

Consequently, all of those who belong to the covenant of grace may be said to participate in the semi-eschatological life, even those who fall away, but they are in a worse position than those outside the covenant, for they are those "who have once been enlightened [baptized], who have tasted the heavenly gift [the Eucharist], and have shared in the Holy Spirit, and have tasted the goodness of the word of God and the powers of the age to come" (Heb. 6:4–5). This last phrase especially reminds us of the eschatological character of the sacraments: the reality (seated with Christ in heavenly places) is not only signified but is actually communicated and certified by the sacraments.

Therefore, the two dangers that a covenantal view of baptism avoids are to collapse the sign into the thing signified, as if the ritual of baptism effected salvation even if one fails to receive the Savior through faith, and to separate the sign and thing signified.

In the former case, baptism is viewed as working in a mechanical or perhaps even magical way: *ex opere operato* (by doing it, it is done). But in this case, the sacraments have their own inherent power distinct from Christ, since they are effective whether one receives Christ or not. It is crucial that we refuse the false dilemma often posed between this mechanical view of the sacraments and a merely symbolic view. Both trade on the mistaken assumption that the sacraments themselves do (or don't do) anything. It was not the ram's head in the Assyrian treaty that cut a covenant, but the Assyrian king, and it is Yahweh the Lord of the covenant who makes his treaty of peace with us and our children. The question therefore is not what the *sacraments* do *to* us, but what *God* does *for* us *with* them. The covenantal background of the biblical sacraments discloses a worldview far removed from the Greek one we have inherited at this point. In the former, sacraments inhabit the world of oaths and bonds, not substances and accidents.

However, at the other end are those who divorce the signs from the reality. Accordingly, one bends over backward to explain away passages in which baptism is explicitly linked to regeneration and forgiveness of sins. Paul speaks of Christ "having cleansed [the church] by the washing of water with the word" (Eph. 5:26). God "saved us, not because of works done by us in righteousness, but according to his own mercy, by the washing of regeneration and renewal of the Holy Spirit" (Titus 3:5). Romans 6 speaks straightforwardly of our baptism into Christ, apparently without any concern to distinguish it from water baptism. Baptism, in fact, is the true circumcision (Col. 2:11–12). The first recorded sermon by a New Testament apostle enjoins, "'Repent and be baptized every one of you in the name of Jesus Christ for the forgiveness of your sins, and you will receive the gift of the Holy Spirit. For the promise is for you and for your children and for all who are far off, everyone whom the Lord our God calls to himself.'... So those who received his word were baptized, and there were added that day about three thousand souls" (Acts 2:38–41).

That there is a distinction between the sign and seal on the one hand and the reality itself can hardly be doubted: in this respect, the new covenant sacraments were the same as the old. Baptism, like circumcision, is a sign and seal of the covenant of grace, not the cause of election, regeneration, and justification. In fact, the same writer who says that the members of the covenant community are beneficiaries of the Spirit's working and have therefore "been enlightened," have "tasted the heavenly gift," and have "tasted the goodness of the word of God and the powers of the age to come" (Heb. 6:4–5) also states that they are in a position analogous to the Israelites in the wilderness: "For good news came to us just as to them, but the message they heard did not benefit them, because they were not united by faith with those who listened" (4:2). Believers must not only *be* baptized, but *receive* the one who was promised to them in their baptism.

Herman Ridderbos adds some helpful remarks in his study of Paul's Epistle to the Romans.

> In the preceding chapters we have been struck time and again by the great significance Paul ascribes to baptism (as well as, though less frequently, to the Lord's Supper) as medium in the appropriation of the salvation given to the church in Christ.... That the expressions "to wash" and "bath of water" refer to baptism cannot be doubted. In both we find baptism, in harmony with the whole of the early Christian proclamation, characterized as the symbol of and means of salvation for the washing away of and cleansing from sin.[27]

Ridderbos points to the many instances in which "baptism is simply qualified as the baptism of the Spirit."[28] He observes that wherever Paul talks about "sealing" (such as 2 Cor. 1:21–22, where God "anointed us, and . . . has also put his seal on us and given us his Spirit in our hearts as a guarantee"), it is linked to baptism.[29] "It is this union with Christ by baptism that Paul intends when in Galatians 3:27 he describes baptism as 'putting on Christ': 'For as many of you as were baptized into Christ have put on Christ.'"[30]

Ridderbos rebukes commentators for spiritualizing "baptism" in these instances. Furthermore, as in the Reformed (covenantal) understanding of the Lord's Supper, the Spirit's work is crucial. How is it that people are still being added to Christ by "dying and rising" with him? Is he forever dying? In baptism Christ's death is not prolonged by bringing it to us; rather, in baptism the Spirit brings us to Christ's death.[31] This is not mere symbolism:

> Baptism is also the means by which communion with the death and burial of Christ comes into being (*dia tou baptismatos*; Rom. 6:4), the place where this union is effected (*en tō baptismati*; Col. 2:12), the means by which Christ cleanses his church (*katharisas tō loutrō*; Eph. 5:26), and God has saved it (*esōsen hēmas dia loutrou*; Titus 3:5), so that baptism itself can be called the washing of regeneration and of the renewing by the Holy Spirit (Titus 3:5). All these formulations speak clearly of the significance of baptism in mediating redemption; they speak of what happens in and by baptism and not merely of what happened before baptism and of which baptism would only be the confirmation.[32]

On the other hand, without faith this baptism does not confer the thing signified.[33] But still, faith doesn't make baptism effective; God does. "Baptism is the means in God's hand, the place where he speaks and acts. On the other hand, this last excludes every suggestion as though baptism were anything in itself and imparted salvation *ex opere operato*."[34]

Passover and Lord's Supper: The Covenant Meal

Examples of meals ratifying treaties are replete in the ancient Near East and in the Old Testament. We recall Moses, Aaron, and the elders at the top of Sinai eating with Yahweh.

We have seen how closely the ritual "cutting" was connected to the making of a covenant. The sign and the thing signified were viewed neither as identical nor in isolation. Just as circumcision could be called "the covenant" because of the close union of the sign and the thing signified, the Passover ritual was itself called "the LORD's passing over," with successive generations called upon to regard themselves as representatively (i.e., covenantally) present with the founding generation, dressed for the road in anticipation of their redemption (Exod. 13:14–16). Furthermore, as we have seen, the ancient treaties had a provision in the case of emergency: the vassal could invoke the name of the suzerain for military deliverance. The invocation of Yahweh has its secular parallel in the secular treaties, whereby the vassal could call upon the name of the suzerain to deliver his people from invading armies. It is no doubt in this context that Israel took up its Passover cup: "I will lift up the cup of salvation and call on the name of the LORD" (Ps. 116:13). Therefore, no part of the covenant can be isolated. It is secured not only by words, but by deeds, not only by a promise spoken, but by a ritual confirmation that certified the pledge. When the Israelites took up the Passover cup, they were calling on God's name for salvation, yet their invocation was not what made the meal a covenantal occasion but rather the meal ratified the covenant.

Not only were the Israelites "baptized into Moses in the cloud and in the sea," says Paul (1 Cor. 10:2); they also "all ate the same spiritual food, and all drank the same spiritual drink. For they drank from the spiritual Rock that followed them, and the Rock was Christ" (vv. 3–4), even though most of those among that generation did not receive that which was signified (v. 5). Paul did not imagine that a literal rock was somehow transubstantiated into the flesh and blood of Jesus Christ. He is not employing the thought-forms of Graeco-Roman mystery religions, but the covenantal language of the ancient Near East as the Old Testament Scriptures had done. So while the rock in the wilderness did not magically become something other than a literal rock, it now became set apart as a sacrament of Christ. The rock and the water that gushed from its side became a sign ratifying the promise, so that those who drank from it were in fact drinking from Christ himself.

Paul represents the sign and the thing signified as distinct yet united: "The cup of blessing that we bless, is it not a participation [koinonia] in the blood of Christ? The bread that we break, is it not a participation in the body of Christ? Because there is one bread, we who are many are one body, for we all partake of the one bread" (vv. 16–17). Thus the union in either case (Moses by shadow and Christ by fulfillment) is covenantal and centers on the act of mediation. Paul goes on to observe the union of sign and signified by contrasting the Lord's Supper with pagan ritual meals in which "those who eat the sacrifices" are "participants in the altar" (v. 18).

In all of this, therefore, two extremes are avoided: the sacerdotal error, which fails to distinguish the sign from the thing signified, and the memorialist error, which fails to recognize the union of the sign and signified. For the former, no real sacrament actually exists: baptism is regeneration, and the bread and wine become the body and blood of Christ. The sign is swallowed by the signified: it no longer exists, despite appearances to the contrary. For the latter also, there really can be no sacrament, for all that is left is the bare sign itself. Baptism and the Lord's Supper may be occasions for a spiritual event by encouraging the participant's powers of reflection, self-examination, and pious memory, but they are not themselves regarded as the occasions of God's powerful witness and work.

At this point, it may be useful to recognize how these two extremes treat Paul's call to self-examination in 1 Corinthians 11, focusing on verses 28–29: "Let a person examine himself, then, and so eat of the bread and drink of the cup. For anyone who eats and drinks without discerning the body eats and drinks judgment on himself." Lifted out of its context, this warning has been taken by sacerdotalism to mean that the condition of worthily receiving the Lord's Supper is the acknowledgment of the presence of Christ's body and blood as the elements themselves (Rome) or at least in, with, and under the elements themselves (Lutheranism). On the other end are those who take it as a warning to rigorous self-examination, to discern whether they have sufficient signs of grace for communing.

The context, however, is all-important, as the warning is couched in a disciplinary argument against idolatry and schism. Many in the Corinthian church were flaunting their Christian liberty in the matter of eating food that had been sacrificed to idols in pagan worship (chap. 8). In addition to the theological divisions, the church was embroiled in social divisions as well. In ancient Roman society, when civic meals were held in homes of the wealthy, the seating arrangement was a grand visual testimony to the caste system. Privileged guests sat at a main table in the dining room, while the others sat in another room or even in the atrium. The best food and wine were served at the head table, and the scraps went to those in the atrium.

Evidently, the "love feasts" in the church had become mirror images of their secular counterparts, even involving drunkenness and gluttony (perhaps even orgies) in the dining hall, while the lowliest went away hungry. No wonder Paul compares their celebration of the Lord's Supper to the Israelites' sitting down to eat and drink and rising up to play around the golden calf (1 Cor. 10:7). It is here that Paul says the cup of blessing and the bread are a participation in the body and blood of Christ (v. 16). While this tells us a great deal about the nature of the Lord's Supper, the main point is that this sacred meal unites the participants into one body (v. 17). They are no longer individuals in an important sense, nor members of a particular social class. They cannot destroy each other over idol meat and social divisions and then pretend to be sharing in the covenant meal. "When you come together, it is not the Lord's supper that you eat. For in eating, each one goes ahead with his own meal. One goes hungry, another gets drunk. What! Do you not have houses to eat and drink in? Or do you despise the church of God and humiliate those who have nothing?" (11:20–22).

Then, just after Paul relates the words of institution, he issues the warning to examine themselves: "Whoever, therefore, eats the bread or drinks the cup of the Lord in an unworthy manner will be guilty of profaning the body and blood of the Lord" (v. 27). One cannot worthily receive the body and blood of Christ in the supper while destroying the body of Christ that is the church. "So then, my brothers, when you come together to eat, wait for one another—if anyone is hungry, let him eat at home—so that when you come together it will not be for judgment" (vv. 33–34).

Wherever there is a discussion of unity in the New Testament, the sacraments are close at hand: "one Lord, one faith, one baptism" (Eph. 4:5); "You are all sons of God through faith in Christ Jesus, for all of you who were baptized into Christ have clothed yourselves with Christ. There is neither Jew nor Greek, slave nor free, male nor female, for you are all one in Christ Jesus" (Gal. 3:26–28 NIV); "Because there is one loaf, we, who are many, are one body, for we all partake of the one loaf" (1 Cor. 10:17 NIV). For this reason, "Nobody should seek his own good, but the good of others" (v. 24 NIV). "The body is a unit, though it is made up of many parts; and though all its parts are many, they form one body. So it is with Christ. For we were all baptized by one Spirit into one body—whether Jews or Greeks, slave or free—and we were all given the one Spirit to drink" (1 Cor. 12:12–13 NIV).

The Lord's Supper, then, is a covenant meal. That means that while it is first of all a ratification of God's pledge to us, it also ratifies our pledge to God and to each other. It has both vertical and horizontal dimensions. In it we receive the body and blood of Christ and are knit together as the body of Christ. As we receive our Living Head by his Spirit, we are made one people. As the bread and wine are a participation (*koinonia*) in Christ, they further bind us in a *koinonia* with each other. One cannot treat the Lord's Supper in an individualistic manner, but only as a covenant meal. Here the hierarchical divisions between poor and rich, slave and free, Jew and Gentile, male and female, are suspended as the rules of "this present age" are overpowered by the melodious strains of "the age to come."

The fact that the Lord's Supper is a covenant meal has tremendous practical implications, as the Reformers realized. In fact, Martin Bucer (the Strasbourg reformer) wrote extensively on the relationship between the Lord's Supper and the communal obligations of rich and poor. In our own day, Karl Deddens observes:

Here we have the very root of diaconal work. The festive spirit in which we celebrate the Lord's Supper is also an occasion for us, in accordance with Lord's Day 38 of the Heidelberg Catechism, to show compassion for the poor. Ideally speaking, it should be possible for the deacons to conduct their work of providing for the poor in the congregation from this [Communion] collection alone. And this ideal would become reality if the festive character of the Lord's Supper came to full expression in our services.[35]

Bucer was right: How would our conduct toward each other be improved if we were a eucharistically oriented people? Could there be churches on either side of the tracks that took no account of each other, being baptized into capitalism instead of Christ? A political party instead of Christ? Racism instead of Christ? Culture Christianity instead of Christ? In many respects, the churches in America today are as divided along socioeconomic, racial, political, and generational lines as the church of Corinth. By being first and foremost the objective place where God meets and blesses his people, the Lord's Supper becomes also the place where a heavenly society on earth, a colony of Christ's kingdom, refuses to suspend its ever-widening encroachment on the kingdom of sin and death. The Word, baptism, and the Lord's Supper form a single island of divinely created unity out of the world's divisive rivalries. Here is the one place where all are one in Christ. It's not the musical style that unites them, the socioeconomic or racial complexion of the community, the age or political orientation. Here, in the pew, at the font, and at the table, only one division really matters: Christ and idols.

The problem with the pietistic version of the Lord's Supper, therefore, is that in its obsession with the individual's inner piety, it loses much of the import of the feast as a sacred meal that actually binds us to Christ and to each other. Instead of viewing it first as God's saving action toward us and then as our fellowship with each other in Christ, we come to see it as just another opportunity to be threatened with the law. Instead of celebrating the foretaste of the marriage supper of the Lamb on Mount Zion, we are still trembling at the foot of Mount Sinai. It is no wonder, then, that there is a diminished interest in frequent communion.

Interestingly, the Synod of Dort of 1578 concluded, "On the day on which the Lord's Supper is celebrated, it will be useful to teach about the sacraments and especially about the hidden character of the Lord's Supper. . . ." Karl Deddens adds:

> If the Lord's Supper were celebrated more often, we should not view such a change as an accommodation to "sacramentalists" who wish to place less emphasis on the service of the Word; rather, we should view it as an execution of Christ's command. . . . There are some people who say: "But the congregation is not asking for more frequent communion!" This may be true, but such a consideration is not determinative. Instead we should be stimulated to engage in some reflection.[36]

Deddens looks to prominent synods in the Netherlands that say there should be "more frequent celebration of the Lord's Supper . . . , pointing to 1 Corinthians 11:17 and other passages by way of support." He complains that certain factors have contributed to a certain weakening of the importance of the Supper: the inordinate length of an overly didactic form, which undermines the festive character of the sacrament, and the influence of pietism in certain circles.

> Under the influence of pietism and mysticism, a sense of "unworthiness" is awakened within them, and they become afraid that they may be "eating and drinking judgment unto themselves." As for those who were still bold enough to go to the table of the Lord, their faces suggest that a funeral is under way rather than a celebration.[37]

We need to make clear to our congregations that they cannot excommunicate themselves. After all, excommunication does mean to keep from communion. Yet we do not have this right to excommunicate ourselves. If members are not being disciplined by the church, they *are* worthy communicants. Paul's warning simply cannot be read as placing the choice of communing in the hands of individuals, who must then determine whether their faith and repentance are equal to the task. After all, the sacrament is given precisely to strengthen weak faith and repentance, to cheer downcast souls with the good news that Christ is sacrificed and raised to the Father's right hand even for them.

Ridderbos rightly recognizes that "worthy eating" in the context of 1 Corinthians has to do with coming to the Supper with understanding and reverence for what is taking place, not in orgies, dissensions, and sacrilege.[38] "The *manducatio indignorum* [the ungodly reception of the bread and wine] and the judgment to which they expose themselves do not abrogate the gracious character of the sacrament."[39] As the preached gospel is good news heard, the Lord's Supper is good news visibly demonstrated for the rest of our senses. God condescends to draw our entire selves, body and soul, around the Savior in heartfelt trust and thankful obedience.

There are many things in the Christian life that are useful and assist us in our walk. Disciplines of prayer and Bible reading, fellowship with believers, evangelism, and social concern are habits that the individual and the church cannot live without. Yet the Word and the sacraments are distinguished from all else as means of *grace*. While prayer is, as the Heidelberg Catechism puts it, "the chief part of gratitude," it is something that moves from us to God, while in the preached Word and the sacraments, the movement is from God to us.

We cannot have grace on ourselves. Only the Great King can confer a blessing on his subjects—especially if that blessing includes adoption of sinners into his own royal family. Nothing that we do—however crucial to our Christian life, can communicate or confirm the promises of God. Only God can do that, and that is why he has instituted the preaching of the gospel and the sacraments as his *modus operandi*. If the place of the sacraments is weakened in our public worship, it is no surprise that we will find

God's people falling back on themselves and their own methods for spiritual health. Our covenant Lord not only knows what we need; he has provided it in the service that he himself has ordained. John Murray rightly insists:

> We partake of Christ's body and blood through the means of the ordinance. We thus see that the accent falls on the faithfulness of God. . . . We must keep in view that salvation is more than its inception. And the sacraments are means through which we are to grow unto the salvation perfected in the last time. It is easy to give way to a spurious kind of spirituality, and regard the sacraments as tending to externalism and ritualism, and not necessary to the highest form of devotion. We must beware of substituting spurious sentiment for obedience.[40]

What Do the Sacraments Do?

Too often the debate over the efficacy of the sacraments is trapped within a philosophical debate over "spirit" and "matter." How can material things like bread and water convey invisible grace? Rome has answered: By obliterating the material thing and replacing it with the spiritual. At the other end, memorialists (in the tradition of the reformer Ulrich Zwingli) have simply concluded that it is impossible for a material thing to convey a spiritual reality. Therefore, baptism must be the token of the believer's promise to be a faithful disciple (or the parents' promise to faithful child-rearing), and the supper must be a rededication to that goal.

But if we think in covenantal rather than philosophical terms, this is the wrong picture from the start. The water in baptism and the bread and wine, joined to the Word by the Spirit, are connected to the heavenly reality they signify and seal as the blood shedding and covenant meals in the ancient Near Eastern worldview. Here there is no contrast between spirit and matter—if there were, the incarnation would have no saving value either. The Assyrian king knew that when he laid his hands on the head of the ram and said, "This is not the head of a ram, but the head of Mati'ilu," he was not making a metaphysical statement about a change of substance *or* reducing the act to a colorful object lesson. He was in that very act certifying the blessings and curses enumerated in the treaty. The head of the ram had undergone a change in such "consecration,"—not from one *substance* to another, but from one *use* to another. It had become a "federal" head, so to speak, representing the political body connected with Mati'ilu. The pact had been sealed.

Furthermore, grace is not an impersonal substance, but a personal attribute. It is not a spiritual tonic that can be passed from one person to another, but is God's own attitude and action that he shows to those who deserve the very opposite. If we think in terms of a king showing favor instead of a substance being passed through a channel, much of the confusion over the sacraments can be overcome.

Unlike Zwingli's view, then, the contrast is not between material and spiritual substance (the former too weak to convey the latter) but between "this age," in which our consciences remain constantly assaulted and Christ has ascended to the right hand of the Father, and "the age to come," which dawns partially in the resurrection of Christ and sending of the Spirit—the other attorney (*parakletos*, John 14:16). His role, as Jesus elaborates it, is also in the form of a covenant lawsuit: to convict and convert (John 16:8–15). The Holy Spirit sent from the ascended Christ will bring believers into communion with the physically absent redeemer (John 14:26; 16:13). "He will glorify me, for he will take what is mine and declare it to you" (16:14). To say that this communion with Christ is spiritual is not to oppose it to matter but to refer it to the Holy Spirit as the divine person who is sent from the Sabbath consummation into this present age, to make new covenant believers participants in the semi-realized new creation. The presence of the Triune God among his people in this age truly is an *adventus*, a coming presence, a presence in absence and absence in presence.

The bread is consecrated and thus set apart by words, says Calvin, but words directed not at the bread but pronounced for the benefit of the hearers. "And this is the conversion which is spoken of by the ancient doctors of the church. . . . In short, consecration is nothing else than a solemn testimony, by which the Lord appoints to us for a spiritual use an earthly and corruptible sign; which cannot take place, unless his command and promise are distinctly heard for the edification of faith."[41] Thus Calvin refuses the false dilemma of either annihilating the sign by the signified (Trent), confusing them (Luther), or separating them (Zwingli).

> A sacrament consists of a visible sign, with which is connected the thing signified, which is the reality of it. . . . But now I must add, that it is not an empty or unmeaning sign which is held out to us, but those who receive this promise by faith are actually made partakers of his flesh and blood. For in vain would the Lord [have] commanded his people to eat *bread*, declaring that *it is his body*, if the effect were not truly added to the figure.[42]

Calvin speaks of the *analogy* of bread and flesh.[43] He reminds us of the Lord's words, that he will not drink this wine with them until the future day: "His disciples will soon be deprived of his presence."[44] And yet, in this supper "he gives an astonishing display of his condescension, in thus letting himself down to the feeble capacity of our flesh for the purpose of invigorating our faith."[45]

Zwingli insisted that a faith that needs such physical props is not true faith, but Calvin and the Reformed confessions sharply disagreed. More important, God himself responded to the incredulity of Abraham by giving him a sign and seal of his promise. The sacraments are remarkable evidence of God's fatherly goodness and condescension to us in our weakness.

The Reformed confessions followed Calvin in his insistence that we hold together two important truths: first, that Christ is ascended bodily and therefore is not present in, much less as, the elements; second, that believers nevertheless receive this same Christ born of Mary and crucified for our sins, but in heaven where he is seated at the Father's right hand. The means is mysterious, and the agent who effects this communion is the Holy Spirit. Some have held that the ascension entails that we only receive Christ according to his divine nature (since it is omnipresent), but this has been rightly rejected as the Nestorian heresy (separating the two natures of Christ in one person). There is no *koinonia* with Christ's divinity (which has always been omnipresent) apart from his humanity, unless one is to favor Nestorianism. This was Calvin's point. And it is also John Murray's in the following:

> We must bear in mind also that all of the virtue accruing from Jesus' death resides in Christ as exalted and glorified. But he is glorified in the body in which he suffered. We may never think of him apart from the body. Hence communion with the body of Christ, or communion of the body of Christ, includes the glorified body, more accurately, communion with him in respect of his glorified body. The virtue proceeding from him is a virtue that proceeds from him as the God-man, and to him in this identity belongs his glorified body. Thus the body performs a function indispensable to the communion of which the Lord's supper is a seal and a means of communication.[46]

The Lord's Supper, therefore, is an irreducible mystery. The Spirit, as Christ promised, takes that which belongs to Christ and gives it to us. He makes us one with Christ, to feed on him as one person. It is the Spirit who not only cries out in our hearts, "Abba, Father!" but who effects our communion even now with the ascended Lord. Therefore, what we receive in the supper is not only confirmation of our own *share* in the sacrifice once offered, but a real *sharing* in the one offered. He is our life now, even as he gave his life then. We cannot receive Christ's benefits apart from receiving Christ himself. It is the office of the Holy Spirit to insert us here and now into the reality of what happened then and there and also into the reality that will be fully realized in the future. The sacraments cannot escape that eschatological dialectic in which we find ourselves: the "already" and the "not yet."

So just as baptism is first of all God's pledge to be our God and the God of our children, the Lord's Supper also is in the first place God's certification of his unyielding oath. The words "given *for you*" in the words of institution are crucial in this regard, Calvin notes. "Therefore, when we approach the holy table, let us not only remember in general that the world has been redeemed by the blood of Christ, but let every one consider for himself that his own sins have been expiated."[47] Through this eating and drinking in faith, "this covenant is ratified, so as to be firm and stable."[48] It is the "new covenant in my blood," and "we infer that a promise is included in the Holy Supper." And Calvin adds, with Zwingli in view, "This refutes the error of those who maintain that faith is not aided, nourished, supported, or increased by the sacraments; for there is always a mutual relation between the *covenant* of God and the faith of men."[49]

By calling the newly instituted supper a participation in his blood of the *new* covenant, Jesus "intended to show that the ancient figures now cease, and give way to a firm and everlasting covenant."[50] The sacraments are not mere badges of profession or "bare signs"; far less are they made sacraments by the piety of the individual or the community. It is neither the action of the signs themselves nor of the people but the action of God that makes the sacraments, in the words of the Westminster Larger Catechism, "effectual means of salvation" (Question 161).

The benefits offered by the sacraments are the same as those offered by the gospel itself: Christ and all his treasures. The sacraments signify and seal to the individual believer the promise that is heard in the preaching of the gospel. In the covenant, says Murray, "We thus see that the accent falls on the faithfulness of God."[51] In fact, "depreciation of baptism insults the wisdom and grace of

God and, more particularly, his faithfulness. He confirms to us the bond of union with himself by adding the seal of baptism, to the end that we may be more firmly established in the faith of his covenant grace."[52]

The Reformed did not, therefore, deny the reality of the presence of Christ in the sacrament but strenuously affirmed the union—not transubstantiation or commingling—of the sign with the thing signified. As Johannes Wollebius (1586–1629) put it, "It is one thing to say that Christ is present in the bread, and quite another to say that he is present in the holy supper."[53] In other words, Reformed theology does hold to the real presence of Christ in the Lord's Supper but does not limit the supper to the elements themselves. In the supper we have to do with the signs *and* the realities they signify. The ring in a wedding does not merely symbolize a union. At least according to the traditional language, we say, "With this ring I thee wed." If this is true in a humanly devised ritual, how much more so in a covenant ceremony in which God's promise has a seal of his own authority attached to it.

The Belgic Confession (1561) emphasizes once again the necessity of the sacraments due to human weakness and anxiety and their nature, consequently, as divine acts (seals, pledges, nourishment, and sustenance) to confirm and uphold our faith.

> We believe that our good God, mindful of our crudeness and weakness, has ordained sacraments for us to seal his promises in us, to pledge his good will and grace toward us, and also to nourish and sustain our faith. He has added these to the Word of the gospel to represent better to our external senses both what he enables us to understand by his Word and what he does inwardly in our hearts, confirming in us the salvation he imparts to us. For they are visible signs and seals of something internal and invisible, by means of which God works in us through the power of the Holy Spirit. So they are not empty and hollow signs to fool and deceive us, for their truth is Jesus Christ, without whom they would be nothing.[54]

It is true that these Reformed statements continue to maintain the view that through the sacraments God actually "imparts to us" inwardly what through them he presents outwardly. In fact, Calvin's successor in Geneva, Theodore Beza, explains the sacraments in relation to the exercise of the keys:

> This however is certain, that the ceremony, which is by God's precept performed in the use of the sacraments, was ratified in heaven: and that thenceforward bread and wine in that sacred action are in quality changed since they are made true symbols of the Lord's body and blood—a thing which they obtain not either of their own nature or by the virtue of certain set pronounced words but by the appointment of the Son of God.... Yet neither transubstantiation nor what they call real conjunction or transfusion or commixture are to be thought of, but the relative or sacramental conjunction of the sign and the thing.... For neither must Christ's body be really present upon earth, in order that we may be partakers of Christ: but rather by the virtue of the Holy Spirit and by faith we must ascend (to Him) to Heaven and there embrace Him that we may sit with Him in Heavenly places.[55]

In his Confession Beza adds, "But the conjunction between the sign and the reality signified is made by the force and power of the Holy Spirit alone." The power is not even in faith, but is rather the power "of God in the Word and in the Sacraments from whom we have faith.... This is the reason why, in the liturgy which the early Church observed, this phrase was in use: 'Lift up your hearts!'"[56]

In more recent times, the Princeton theologian A. A. Hodge has raised the issue of presence, with an implicit criticism of those within the tradition who understand "spiritual presence" in a non-Reformed (i.e., Zwinglian) manner:

> If he is not present really and truly, then the sacrament can have no interest or real value to us. It does not do to say that this presence is only spiritual, because that phrase is ambiguous. If it means that

the presence of Christ is not something objective to us, but simply a mental apprehension or idea of him subjectively present to our consciousness, then the phrase is false. Christ as an objective fact is as really present and active in the sacrament as are the bread and wine, or the minister or our fellow-communicants by our side. If it means that Christ is present only as he is represented by the Holy Ghost, it is not wholly true, because Christ is one Person and the Holy Ghost another, and it is Christ who is personally present. . . . It does not do to say that the divinity of Christ is present while his humanity is absent, because it is the entire indivisible divine-human Person of Christ which is present.[57]

Christ promised his enduring presence to his church. "But what do we mean by 'presence'? It is a great mistake to confuse the idea of 'presence' with that of nearness in space. . . . 'Presence,' therefore, is not a question of space; it is a relation" (emphasis added).[58] This is the crux of the Reformed understanding of the eucharistic presence. As grace is not a question of substance but divine acceptance, the sacramental presence is not a question of space but of covenant ratification and assurance. It is here, at the font and the communion table, as well as in the pew as we hear the gospel preached, that the question is finally settled for us: God is present; he is near. And he comes in peace.

Finally, the Lord's Supper not only looks to the past in memory and receives in the present, but it also announces the return of Christ: "For as often as you eat this bread and drink the cup, you proclaim the Lord's death until he comes" (1 Cor. 11:26). In the supper, not only God, but the people who have called on his name, announce prophetically the coming of the kingdom in weakness (the Lord's death) with a view to the Lord's kingdom in glory and power. As this resurrection has secured the new life of the "inner man," it guarantees the resurrection of each person's body. The Holy Spirit has been sent as a "deposit guaranteeing our inheritance until the redemption of those who are God's possession" (Eph. 1:14 NIV). And it is this Holy Spirit who brings to us the reality (Christ and the new creation) that he outwardly promises and pledges through Word and sacrament.

Herman Ridderbos notes particularly of Paul's concept:

> It is not merely a subjective recalling to mind, but an active manifestation of the continuing and actual significance of the death of Christ. "Proclaim" in this respect has a prophetic, declaratory significance. . . . Everything is directed not only toward the past, but also toward the future. It is the proclamation that in the death of Christ the new and eternal covenant of grace has taken effect, if still in a provisional and not yet consummated sense.[59]

As such the supper is also "the foundation and criterion for the unity of the church as the new people of God."[60] Key to the Reformed conception is the eschatological role of the Holy Spirit in the Eucharist. "For Paul," writes Geerhardus Vos, "the Spirit was regularly associated with the world to come, and from the Spirit thus conceived in all His supernatural and redemptive potency the Christian life receives throughout its specific character."[61]

This once again points up the close association between the covenant word and its sacramental ratification. In the older communion liturgies, this dimension is given voice in the people's confession, "Christ has died, Christ is risen, Christ will come again." The objective facts of Christ's own history—that is, the gospel—create worthy receivers of the sacrament, and the sacrament nourishes and sustains faith in that saving message.

"Where does this faith come from?" "The Holy Spirit creates it in our hearts by the preaching of the holy gospel," according to the Heidelberg Catechism (Question and Answer 65), "and confirms it by the use of the holy sacraments." The Lord's Supper is God's own confirmation of his everlasting covenant, and in our communal reception of this gift we proclaim and, in fact, exhibit before the watching world the reality of the age to come in this present age.

9

New Covenant Obedience

So far we have emphasized that the Old Testament it-self presents us with two distinct types of covenants: law and promise, the latter serving as the basis for the covenant of grace. To be sure, we can inherit the blessings of Abraham only on the basis of an unconditional divine oath, given our condition in sin. Nevertheless, salvation has come to us not by the setting aside of the law but by the fulfilling of it. While we inherit salvation by grace, it first had to be won for us by the most thorough obedience. In a very real sense, we are saved by works: Christ's. Yet we receive this salvation by faith in his saving work on our behalf. So the law is upheld—and not only the law, but the covenant of works, which commanded, "Do this and you shall live." Christ did fulfill the divine requirements and was raised to the right hand of the Father. Because of his victory, we too will be vindicated at the great cosmic trial. We already have God's word on it in the gospel of free justification, which belongs to us even now, as confirmed by our baptism and participation in the Lord's Supper.

But is there any other sense in which the law is upheld other than its having been fulfilled for us in Christ? If the Sinai covenant is no longer in force and we are "under grace"—that is, under a covenant of promise rather than of law—is any principle of law excluded for the New Testament believer? Do we ignore all ethical teaching in the Old Testament as nonbinding and accept only those commands that we find in the New Testament? What is the place, if any, for the law in the Christian life?

If we are asking this question, we can be assured that we have correctly understood the gospel as good news. After several chapters of expounding the message that sinners are justified by faith apart from works, Paul asks in Romans 6:1, "What shall we say then? Are we to continue in sin that grace may abound?" If the preaching of the gospel we have heard leads us to wonder whether we can dispense with the law altogether, then it has been correctly heard. But Paul's answer to the question, of course, is a resounding "No!" His response is not like that of a law covenant. In other words, he does not say, "If you do continue in sin, you will suffer the consequences (loss of rewards or even loss of salvation)." Rather, his reply is that it is *impossible* for those who have been baptized into Christ's death to remain in the tomb; they have been brought forth by the Spirit into new life. The good news just keeps getting better and better, and it is enough to save us from not only the guilt but the tyranny of our sins as well. But does this new obedience just happen without our needing to follow any prescribed code? Wouldn't such a view of the law as normative mean a relapse to the killing letter of the law when the Spirit has made us alive in Christ?

Using the Law Lawfully

A lot of discussion about the role of the law in the new covenant gets off to the wrong start by a failure to make important distinctions. As a result, it is easy for different parties simply to take sides for or against the normative use of the law for Christians. What are some of those distinctions, then, that we need to recognize?

* First, it is important to bear in mind the difference between the law itself and a covenant of law.

Historically, exegetes have (justifiably, in my view) understood "law" and "gospel" on two levels: (1) the principle of law (personal fulfillment of its stipulations) distinct from the principle of promise/gospel; and (2) the old covenant (promise) in relation to the new covenant (fulfillment). So one could say that the gospel is revealed in the "law," taken as the Old Testament's Pentateuch, while nevertheless affirming that law (commands) and promises are distinguished even to the point of stark opposition when it comes to the question of our justification before God.

"Law" as a principle simply refers to anything that God commands. Anything that comes to us from God in the form of *imperatives* (things to do or not do) is law. This can be in the form of the Ten Commandments, the elaborate specifications of the temple furnishings, Jesus's teaching on divorce and remarriage, or instructions for life in the Spirit in Galatians 5:16–24. The Old and New Testaments do not differ in the slightest in issuing commands, so we cannot simply equate the former with law and the latter with promise. From the biblical point of view, there is nothing wrong with commandments; they are God's expression of his own moral character. What the Scriptures labor to demonstrate is not that there are no normative laws for Christians, but that there is no way that we, being who we are, can become heirs of God's kingdom by keeping them. Once we exclude the possibility of being related to God according to a covenant of law, we still have to determine from Scripture whether we are obligated to God's laws.

Even the covenant of Sinai, as enshrined in Deuteronomy, contains elements of promise. This is why we have to be careful with our categories. One can say there is gospel in the law if by that one means there is gospel (in the first sense above, "good news") in the Old Testament—including the parts of the Old Testament identified as "the Law" (in the second sense). Further, one can say there is law in the gospel if one means there are commands (first sense) in the New Testament (the gospel in the second sense). While the *basis* of the covenant of grace is God's unconditional, electing, and redeeming grace (no confusion of law and gospel), there are clearly, in its *administration*, both commands and promises. It is when we speak of the basis of the covenant that law and gospel are strictly opposed. That is, law and gospel are distinguished and even opposed whenever we mean by these terms a *covenant* of law and a *covenant* of promise.

With this in mind, we can even find gospel promises in Deuteronomy, for example, as Kline points out.

> Nevertheless, when we have in view the particular verbal and ritual process of ratification that transpired on a certain day on the plains of Moab and by which the Deuteronomic Covenant was constituted a covenant, then we must say that this covenant was based on Israel's oath of allegiance rather than on a bilateral oath. Certainly there is nothing at this point similar to the theophanic action of Genesis 15. Nor is the place occupied by the divine oath in Deuteronomy 32:40 the same as that of the central and constitutive divine oath in the covenant later given to David (see, e.g., II Sam. 7:14ff.; Pss. 89:4[3]; 132:11).[1]

In other words, some elements of promise owing to the Abrahamic covenant are still in force, but the Sinai pact itself is in form and substance a law covenant. Joshua 24 describes Israel's renewal of this covenant as a "statute and an ordinance," supporting the view that it is a law covenant.[2] Kline adds:

> The Sinaitic administration, called "covenant" in the Old Testament, Paul interpreted as in itself a dispensation of the kingdom inheritance quite opposite in principle to inheritance guaranteed by promise: "For if the inheritance is by law, it is no longer by promise" and "the law is not of faith; but, the man that doeth them shall live in them" (Gal. 3:18a, RSV, and v. 12, ARV; cf. Lev. 18:5). Calvin reflects the contrast in principle brought out by Paul when

he says that although promises of mercy are found in the law taken as a whole ("the whole law"), they are borrowed elements there and "are not to be considered as part of the law when the mere nature of the law is the subject of discussion."[3]

This distinction that Calvin invites is basically one between "the entire Mosaic economy . . . and the Sinaitic Covenant as a specific legal whole. And we must recognize that, according to Paul, it was this specific covenantal entity, the Sinaitic Covenant as such, that made inheritance to be by law, not by promise—not by faith, but by works."[4] Both Calvin and Kline, in other words, are making a distinction between the law in the broader and narrower senses. (This is one of those rare occasions when theologians and clothing designers bear at least superficial similarities.)

▲ *A second action we can take in determining the role of the law in the new covenant is to distinguish between the different sorts of law we find in Scripture: the moral, the civil, and the ceremonial.*

If the Sinai covenant is now obsolete, then the specific commands contained in that portion of Scripture are to be recognized as having been given to Israel when God took the nation into his care. It is true that the Ten Commandments given at Mount Sinai were, strictly speaking, directed to Israel. The rest of us "overheard" them. Furthermore, these commandments were not given in isolation, but were followed by the giving of the laws establishing the theocracy: Israel's sociopolitical and cultic life. Civil laws concerning fences on roofs and treatment of land, aliens, and prisoners are obviously in force only so long as the theocracy itself exists. Ceremonial laws governing worship, including specific purification rites, distinctions between clean and unclean animals as well as people, and the temple, priesthood, and sacrifices are similarly "canonical" only as long as the theocracy stands. Peter's vision of the clean and unclean animals, which leads to his full acceptance of the gentile mission, is a classic example of the fact that the old covenant has now been rendered obsolete. The strict purity laws, which symbolized the separation of Jews from Gentiles, are no longer in force (Acts 10:9–43). It is not without warrant, therefore, that Calvin (like the Lutheran reformer Philip Melanchthon) followed many church fathers in distinguishing three types of old covenant law: the moral, the civil, and the ceremonial.

The moral law, summarized in the Ten Commandments, is inscribed on our consciences by virtue of our being created in God's image (Romans 1–3). While the Ten Commandments served as the nucleus for the other laws governing the theocracy, many of them can be found in civilizations even before the founding of Israel (the famous Code of Hammurapi serving as a classic example). Furthermore, the precepts of this moral law are elaborated in the New Testament. In the process, far from being less demanding, the New Testament intensifies the requirements by emphasizing their internal significance. This is meant both to show us our hypocrisy in thinking that we have kept the law merely by conforming outwardly and to guide those upon whose hearts the Spirit has written it as part of his new covenant blessing.

Jesus's summary of the two tables of the Ten Commandments as loving God and our neighbor with our whole hearts demonstrates the continuity between the covenants in terms of what God requires (Matt. 22:37 and parallels). In terms of the moral law, God's expectations have not changed at all from the Old to the New Testament, since God himself cannot change his own moral dispositions. Paul's marvelous description of life in the Spirit and the fruit of the Spirit is simply an elaboration of the inner significance of the moral law: loving God and neighbor.

Some time ago, while waiting to join the rest of our panel for a radio discussion, a rabbi and I began discussing our common ground and differences. The latter, he said, centered on the way our two religions came to the law. For Jews, he said, sin is an explicit violation of a commandment—something that one does with one's hands, while Jesus taught that the commandments could be broken already in one's heart. I would challenge the rabbi's reading of the Old Testament itself, where the goal of the law is obedience from the heart and not merely in outward behavior. Think especially of the numerous times the prophets excoriate the people for an externalism that avoids the deeper motives and intentions of the law. Yet it is certainly true that Jesus and his apostles intensify this internalization of love's prescriptions. Jesus did not make the law easier, but more difficult. When Jesus gave his Sermon on the Mount, corresponding to Moses's giving of the law at Sinai, all notions of a "kinder, gentler" Moses in the person of Jesus are put to flight (Matt. 5:17–6:4; 19:1–12, 16–30).

Where both Jewish and Christian covenant theology agree is that piety is directed to others—God and our neighbor, not chiefly toward ourselves. Many Christians today associate words like *piety, devotion, spirituality,* and *Christian life* with things a believer does in private. "How's your walk?" is shorthand really for asking how well you are keeping up with your personal Bible reading, devotions, and other spiritual disciplines. None of these are wrong, of course. In fact, Jesus modeled getting alone regularly to read Scripture and pray. Nevertheless, a covenantal orientation places much more emphasis on what we do together, with each other and for each other. This in no way entails that we do what we should, but there is an interrelational focus in covenant theology that is different from individualistic pieties. As University of Edinburgh historical theologian David F. Wright notes, "The piety Calvin advocated was largely communal, churchly. There is much here about 'frequenting the sermons' and sharing in the Lord's supper, but very little about individual devotional reading of the Bible or daily routines of prayer, let alone group Bible studies or prayer groups."[5] It is not that these were not present, but that the two tables of the Law—love of God and love of neighbor—rather than extrabiblical routines, could be received as binding on God's people.

Therefore, in *content* the New Testament fills out the meaning of the moral law in terms of attitudes, dispositions, and motives—

rather than simply outward action. And in terms of *responsibility*, new covenant believers have an even greater obligation, for the Spirit has circumcised their hearts and not just their flesh, so that now love of God and neighbor stands as an even more "reasonable service" that we owe in view of the "mercies of God" (Rom. 12:1 KJV). So while the civil and ceremonial laws pertain exclusively to the theocracy and are no longer binding, the moral law is still in force. It is not only clearly elucidated in the pages of Scripture; it is inscribed in the conscience of every human being.

   ◄ *Third, to determine the role of the law in the new covenant, we*
   must distinguish between the three uses of this moral law.

Sometimes in Scripture the law is regarded as a curb to criminal behavior. Even a pagan emperor known for his persecution of the church can be called "God's servant," as in Romans 13:

> Let every person be subject to the governing authorities. For there is no authority except from God, and those that exist have been instituted by God. Therefore whoever resists the authorities resists what God has appointed, and those who resist will incur judgment. For rulers are not a terror to good conduct, but to bad.
>
> verses 1–3

Because this law is known at least in a fragmentary way by unbelievers, it can cause evildoers to think twice in the light of civil penalties. This is often called the *civil* use of the law.

The second use of the law is to drive us to Christ by showing us our sin; hence, it is often called the *pedagogical* use. It is in this sense that Paul says, "I would not have known what it is to covet if the law had not said, 'You shall not covet.'... Apart from the law, sin lies dead.... So the law is holy, and the commandment is holy and righteous and good" (Rom. 7:7–13) even though it brings only bad news and death because of our sin.

The third use of the law is often called its *normative* use because it provides norms for the Christian life. This use of the law is only for believers, since the threat of the law's curse is removed. No longer capable of condemning us, the law sees us in Christ as those who have fulfilled it, and instead of standing over against us, it is written on our heart. The law becomes a delight even though we continue to offend in thought, word, and deed (Rom. 7:21–24).

Law and love cannot be set in opposition, for as we have seen, they go together in both the ancient Near Eastern treaties and in Scripture. The law is summarized by our Lord as loving God and neighbor, and Paul has no other law in mind when he speaks of love being a fulfillment of the law (Rom. 13:10). Interestingly, he repeats this just before his passage on the fruit of the Spirit (Gal. 5:14). So we cannot say that the new covenant replaces obligations of law with those of love, since the law had always been regarded as the specification of love's duties. We have been set free from the personal obligation of fulfilling the law as a condition for eternal life so that, freed from its curse, we can be liberated for the first time to truly love and serve others, which is to obey the law in its deepest intent.

Hopefully we can see from these examples that such distinctions are not deductions from systematic theology but arise naturally and organically from Scripture itself. Furthermore, not only Calvin and the Reformed tradition but Luther and Lutheranism insisted on all three uses of the law, including the abiding significance of the law as the norm for the believer's life.[6]

With these distinctions in mind, how are we to understand *conditions* in the new covenant? Just as there is law (in the broader sense, i.e., commandments) in the gospel (in the narrower sense, i.e., the New Testament), there are obvious conditions in the new covenant. But how can there be conditions in a covenant of promise: an absolute, unchangeable, unconditional divine oath that God swore?

Covenant and Conditionality

Anchored in the covenant of redemption—that eternal pact between the persons of the Trinity—the promise identified with Abraham, David, and the new covenant is *in its essence* unchangeable, inviolable, and without reference to the obedience or disobedience of human agents apart from that obedience of our Mediator, Jesus Christ. In this eternal covenant, we are beneficiaries but not partners. God will save his elect, overcoming every obstacle in his way, including us. Nevertheless, the covenant of grace in its *administration* involves conditions. It is a covenant made with believers and their children. Not everyone in the covenant of grace is elect: the Israel below is a larger class than the Israel above. Some Israelites heard the gospel in the wilderness and responded in faith, while others did not—and the writer to the Hebrews uses this as a warning also to the New Testament heirs of the same covenant of grace (Heb. 4:1–11).

The New Testament lays before us a vast array of conditions for final salvation. Not only initial repentance and faith, but perseverance in both, demonstrated in love toward God and neighbor, are part of that holiness without which no one shall see the Lord (Heb. 12:14). Such holiness is not simply definitive—that is, it belongs not only to our justification, which is an imputed rather than imparted righteousness, but to our sanctification, that inner renewal by the Spirit.

Jesus made it amply clear that the sheep will be distinguished from the goats on the last day by marks of their profession (Matthew 24). It is important to remember, however, that the sheep are apparently unaware of their having fed the hungry, clothed the naked, and cared for the poor and those in prison, while the goats insisted that they had. Holiness, which is defined by love of God and neighbor, is usually something that is seen by others rather than by us. Nevertheless, it is the indispensable condition of our glorification: no one will be seated at the heavenly banquet who has not begun, however imperfectly, in new obedience. There are those who "have once been enlightened [baptized], who have tasted the heavenly gift [the Supper], and have shared in the Holy Spirit, and have tasted the goodness of the word of God and the powers of the age to come" who nevertheless fall away (Heb. 6:4–5).

Does this not seriously compromise the good news of an unconditional promise that we have labored to distinguish from a covenant of works? This is a terribly important question, especially since there seems to be so much confusion in our day over how to take these sober warnings in Scripture. The first order of business is to reexamine careful distinctions.

The first distinction is between justification on one hand and sanctification and glorification on the other. Too often we use *justification* and *salvation* interchangeably, so the suggestion that we are justified without any condition other than faith leads some to conclude that it is the only condition of salvation. However, salvation is understood broadly in Scripture to encompass the whole work of God in restoring his fallen creation.

As we have seen, justification can only be through faith in Christ, not by works. True, there are other conditions that precede faith in Christ. Some readers can recall their conversions. Someone gave them a Bible, another person brought them to church, and once there, others extended fellowship. Then one day the hearing of God's Word produced its intended effect by the Spirit. Details vary enormously, of course, but they are all conditions, without which (humanly speaking) one would not have come to know the Savior.

We must ordinarily hear the law and come under its convicting power, turning from self to Christ. Our hearts must be changed, so that where we once resisted the Word of God, we now accept it. Yet none of this belongs to either the grounds or means of justification. In the words of the Westminster Confession, believers are justified "not for anything wrought in them or done by them, but for Christ's sake alone" (chap. 11). To say that certain things have to happen before we are justified is not to say that any of these things are instruments in our justification. *Conditions* are not *instruments*.

Those who are justified are being sanctified and will one day be glorified. Therefore, it is impossible to say that one can be justified and yet still remain "dead in trespasses and sins" (Eph. 2:1)."The natural person," not the believer, rejects "the things of the Spirit of God, for they are folly to him, and he is not able to understand them because they are spiritually discerned" (1 Cor. 2:14). Everyone who is buried with Christ in the likeness of his death is raised with him in the likeness of his resurrection (Rom. 6:4–5). Returning to spiritual blindness and death is an impossibility for those who are in Christ. It is in this light that we can say that only those who are being sanctified will be glorified. That inward holiness that God requires is not to be confused with justification, but it also cannot be separated from it. Those who are justified will enter heaven with new hearts that delight in God's law, and no one who despises God's law will enter its sacred precincts.

Second, we must distinguish between conditions within a law covenant and conditions within a promise covenant. The law could command, but it could not give what it required. That was not its purpose (Gal. 3:21). It could only declare those who *fulfilled* it to be righteous before God. To speak of conditionality in a law covenant, then, is to follow the formula, "Do this and you will live; fail to do it and you will surely die." Here, the law promises blessing upon fulfillment of the covenant's stipulations.

However, in a covenant of promise things are radically different. To be sure, the requirements of the law themselves do not change, but the basis for acceptance does. In Jeremiah 31, God one-sidedly pledges to replace our stony hearts with hearts of flesh and write his law on them, so that we will delight in his commands—but this itself is the result of his having forgiven us all our sins by grace alone. Everything that God *requires* in this covenant is also *given* by God! It is not simply the case that he promises to forgive our sins and then leaves us to sort out our own stony hearts and rebellious ways. The salvation that he promises and provides is total, leaving nothing for us to achieve through our own strength. Not only justification, but regeneration, sanctification, and everything requisite for our being glorified has been included in this unconditional promise.

Therefore, the covenant of grace is unconditional with respect to its basis, resting on the eternal covenant of redemption. Just as Abraham and his wayward heirs and David and his notoriously wicked sons (the apple doesn't fall far from the tree) could not get in God's way of fulfilling his plan of redemption through them, God's eternal covenant of redemption will be realized in each of the elect despite all obstacles. Not one of his sheep will be lost; all will persevere to the end. So now a condition such as "all who persevere to the end shall be saved" can come to us not as a threat—a condition that somehow we have to meet if we ever hope to attain our own salvation—but rather as a condition that we know God himself will work out for us and within us according to his own good pleasure (Phil. 2:13).

Yet not everyone who belongs to the covenant community will persevere to the end. Some are weeds sown among the wheat, seeds that fell on rocky soil or that is choked by the weeds. Some branches do not bear fruit and are broken off. Again, this should be threatening only to those who in fact do fall away, those who like Esau forfeit their birthright for a paltry alternative. It is possible to be in the covenant externally but not to actually be united to Christ through faith.

It is not the faithful who gather together to participate in the weekly covenant renewal ceremony who should be threatened by a final excommunication on the last day, but those who are unrepentant and unbelieving among us. This is why Hebrews 6 follows its dire warning with these comforting words: "Though we speak in this way, yet in your case, beloved, we feel sure of better things—things that belong to salvation" (v. 9). Those who apostatize from the faith are members of the covenant community and have benefited remarkably from the Spirit's work among them and even, in some mysterious way, within them, through his Word and sacraments. Yet all of this covenantal solidarity cannot itself bring with it "things that belong to salvation." God works faith in our hearts by the preaching of the gospel and confirms it by the sacraments, but not all who hear that gospel and receive its sacraments actually receive the one who gives himself through them. Those who are repentant and trust in Christ can know that these warnings do not pertain to them. Our Lord never quenches a flickering candle or breaks off a bruised reed.

What the Law *Still* Cannot Do

When we reduce the gospel to forgiveness of sins, we miss out on the "height and depth" of what God has accomplished for us in the new covenant. We can easily ignore, on one hand, the demands that continue to be placed on us and, on the other, the liberating good news that sanctification is not finally up to us. Many Christians confess that justification and forgiveness of sins are by grace alone through faith alone in Christ alone, assuming that this has reference to an initial act. One "gets saved" by grace, but then the Christian life is a matter of stepping in and out of God's everlasting blessings based on performance. Paul had something like this in mind in Galatians 3:2–3: "Let me ask you only this: Did you receive the Spirit by works of the law or by hearing with faith? Are you so foolish? Having begun by the Spirit, are you now being perfected by the flesh?"

This problem easily emerges, in the form of both antinomianism (i.e., the belief that we are free from all obligations to the law) and legalism (i.e., the law as the means of attaining life), just at the point where we begin to talk about the third use of the law—the law as a guide for Christian behavior. No Christian really believes that the Christian life is to be entirely without any norms whatsoever. In fact, although I was raised in circles where we were told that the Ten Commandments had no bearing on

New Testament believers, a score of nonbiblical cultural taboos rushed in to fill the vacuum. Since we thought that Christians who had wine with their meal probably were not Christians (at least victorious ones), these norms did in fact function more "legalistically" than the Ten Commandments do in churches that accept the moral law.

So if we all agree that Christians as individuals and communities require certain standards for how we should live, the question is whether those norms should originate with us or with God. I evidently still have not been married long enough to overcome my penchant for buying presents for my wife that she doesn't actually want. Instead, I often will buy her what I want her to have or think she wants. When I don't get the response I'd like, my response (even if unstated) is frequently something like this: "Look, if you tell me what you want every time Christmas or your birthday rolls around, I'll never be able to be spontaneous and creative in expressing my love for you." Of course, there are countless ways in a given day in which I could express my love in spontaneous and creative ways, but it is not, at the end of the day, a sign of love but of selfishness if I do not consider her likes and dislikes when it comes to presents. How much more are our pretensions to pleasing God actually displeasing when we willfully determine for ourselves—out of our own desire for exercising spontaneity and creativity—what kind of response to his grace brings him joy. My wife is a sinner just as I am, but God is holy. He has not simply revealed personal preferences, but the law that expresses his own moral character. He has not commanded anything of us that is not required by the core of his very being. His commands never spring from a whim, but come from a will that is rooted in his unchanging nature.

If the preceding arguments are true—namely, that God has given his law, his law is the very impress of his unchanging character, and the New Testament commands expand and deepen rather than withdraw or curtail that moral law—then it follows that we are no less obligated than the Israelites to obey everything that God has commanded in his moral law. This moral law can be easily distinguished from the ceremonial and civil laws that are inextricably connected to the Mosaic theocracy, and is still in force for both believers and even for all human beings, since it is preserved in their conscience from creation.

Having defended this third use of the law, it is equally important to remind ourselves what the law can and cannot do even according to this third use. After all, the impression can sometimes be given that while the law cannot justify us, it can sanctify us. We may carefully distinguish law and gospel in justification but then confuse them in our treatment of the Christian life, as if those who are now justified can derive strength from the law for their homeward journeys. This, however, is as impossible in sanctification as in justification. In the various uses of the law, its basic function never changes: it commands; that is its office. The law (considered as God's "command") never does more than that. Whether the Decalogue or Paul's teaching on the fruit of the Spirit, such moral instruction can guide, can tell us what our gracious Father calls us to do, but it can never animate our hearts or motivate our hands. That is why obedience is the fruit of the *Spirit.* Jeremiah's prophecy, remember, is not only of forgiveness of sins but of a total restoration, beginning with regeneration and a new obedience.

This heartfelt trust and obedience was God's intention all along. God created us in his image, as his own people, to reflect his glory and to rule over the rest of creation faithfully in his name until the whole earth would become full of his glory. We were created strong, not weak; faithful, not unfaithful; righteous, not wicked; God-centered, not self-centered. The fall created a break, a fissure, a departure. Nevertheless, God could not change his moral nature or the expectations he had for humanity as his image-bearers. God would not stop until he completely restored that image and was able to commune with humanity as a full partner again.

It is in this light that we read in Psalm 40 of a "new song" put in the mouth of the psalmist.

> Sacrifice and offering you have not desired,
>   but you have given me an open ear [lit., "ears that you have
>   dug out for me"].
> Burnt offering and sin offering
>   you have not required.
> Then I said, "Behold, I have come;
>   in the scroll of the book it is written of me:
> I desire to do your will, O my God;
>   your law is within my heart."
>
> verses 6–8

This is a consistent refrain in the Prophets as well: forgiveness is good, but obedience is better. And then we come to Hebrews 10:

> For since the law has but a shadow of the good things to come instead of the true form of these realities, it can never, by the same sacrifices that are continually offered every year, make perfect those who draw near. Otherwise, would they not have ceased to be offered, since the worshipers, having once been cleansed, would no longer have any consciousness of sin? But in these sacrifices there is a reminder of sin every year. For it is impossible for the blood of bulls and goats to take away sins.
>
> Consequently, when Christ came into the world, he said,
> "Sacrifices and offerings you have not desired,
>   but a body have you prepared for me;
> in burnt offerings and sin offerings
>   you have taken no pleasure.
> Then I said, 'Behold, I have come to do your will, O God,
>   as it is written of me in the scroll of the book.'"

When he said above, "You have neither desired nor taken pleasure in sacrifices and offerings and burnt offerings and sin offerings" (these are offered according to the law), then he added, "Behold, I have come to do your will." He abolishes the first in order to establish the second. And by that will we have been sanctified through the offering of the body of Jesus Christ once for all.

verses 1–10

The argument is plain enough. The main point is not only that the old covenant worship was incapable of taking away sins, true as that is, but that forgiveness itself is not the only covenantal blessing that is promised in the new covenant, which the writer then rehearses again for us by quoting Jeremiah 31—the law written on our hearts, as well as forgiveness (Heb. 10:15–17). At the heart is his announcement not only that our sins have been forgiven once and for all by Christ's death, but that obedience has finally been rendered once and for all by our covenant head, so that God can finally have us back as those who, in his Son, are themselves a fragrant offering. In other words, this passage emphasizes that what God really wants is not a guilt-offering of animals for transgressions of his covenant, but a thank-offering of human beings themselves in obedience to the covenant. The law made provisions for *violations* but could never bring about the true *forgiveness* of all sins and the *obedient lives* of thanksgiving, which are his ultimate delight. Instead, every time an Israelite packed up the family for the trip to Jerusalem on the Day of Atonement, the bleating sheep or goat they brought with them was a constant reminder of their sins.

Ultimately, God wants to put our sins behind us—and him—and restore us to his favor. Moreover, he wants to bury our sins so that he can raise us to new life, so that he can finally have a family that delights in his will. The law not only could not bring ultimate forgiveness; "the law made nothing perfect" (Heb 7:19). The gospel brings both ultimate forgiveness and perfection in its wake: forgiveness now and the beginnings of that perfection that will be ours in glory.

So in this announcement there is a twofold message of good news beyond forgiveness. First, Christ's sacrifice included his life as well as his death, his daily obedience to the Father's covenantal will as well as his willingness to be impaled on the cross. Second, because Christ's life and death are reckoned to us, the Spirit can now work in us that obedience which the law could never accomplish. "He abolishes the first"—the old covenant—"in order to establish the second"—the new covenant. No longer bleating sheep and goats, but a body—the body of our Lord himself—is prepared for this new covenant sacrifice: a sacrifice of obedience *and* death. But it is a sacrifice that, by forever settling our acceptance before God, goes on to bring about that renewal of human hearts and new obedience promised in Jeremiah 31. To be sure, our obedience is never complete. Inner renewal and renovation are always in process, falling short of that holiness of heart and life that we will enjoy in our glorification. Nevertheless, we *have* died with Christ and we *have* been raised with him in newness of life. These new covenant blessings cannot be reversed.

The irony in all of this is that the very law that promised life upon obedience brought death (Rom. 7:10). The regime of law could never bring about the obedience it required. This is absolutely counterintuitive. In every religion, and for the average person we meet on the street, the purpose of religion is to make people better. Every person carries around within himself or herself the tarnished recognition of the covenant of works, the law written on the conscience. The gospel, by contrast, comes as news from outside of us, brought to us by a messenger. It is not natural to us, but utterly foreign. Law cannot bring life. Religion is the house of bondage. Yet the gospel brings good news about what someone else has done for us.

> There is therefore now no condemnation for those who are in Christ Jesus. . . . For God has done what the law, weakened by the flesh, could not do. By sending his own Son in the likeness of sinful flesh and for sin, he condemned sin in the flesh, in order

that the righteous requirement of the law might be fulfilled in us, who walk not according to the flesh but according to the Spirit.

Romans 8:1–4

God himself did what the law itself could never do. The law commands, but only God can save.

This is not just good news for the newly converted, but for the mature believer. As John Murray says, "The law cannot do any more in sanctification than it did in justification."[7] It is no more the office of the law (even according to its third use) to empower us for holiness than to raise us from the dead and put us right before God in the first place. The only source of life and power in the Christian life is the same as it was at the very first: the good news that God has done what the law (and our obedience) could never do. Thus, we always respond to the *law* (in its third use) as those who have been saved and are being saved and will be saved according to God's *promise*, within a covenant of grace. Because we are in Christ, God's law, as the expression of his righteous verdict upon our lives, concurs with the gospel in delivering the judgment, "Not guilty." And now, acknowledging us to be right before God, that same law charts our course, revealing God's unchanging will in which he delights more than sacrifice. Forgiveness is great, but obedience is greater. A guilt offering is necessary for the remission of sins, but a thank offering is something that God treasures above all else. It is in view of God's mercies (the indicative) that we offer ourselves as living sacrifices to God (Rom. 12:1–2).

So the good news is that if you are in Christ, you are a new creature. The indicative (i.e., the good news of what God has done—"the mercies of God") drives the imperatives (i.e., the law in its third use). You have not inherited forgiveness and justification by grace only to have your sanctification determined by a covenant of law. The irony is preserved: the law covenant leads to condemnation, while the promise covenant leads to the very obedience that the law requires but could never elicit. On the other hand, if you are living in open rebellion against the promises of

God and do not delight in his law inwardly, then the inheritance does not belong to you even if you have been incorporated visibly into the covenant community. The gospel is greater than we ever imagined, and the judgment is severe for those who reject the realities it brings into our lives.

An illustration will help us to bring these threads together. Imagine a new sailboat with all of the latest gadgets. Equipped with satellite technology, the sailboat can plot the course to your destination. It can even signal alarm when you veer from its coordinates. Relying on the impressive gear, you venture out into the open waters under full sail until eventually the winds die down and you come to a dead calm. The radio warns that a squall is suddenly approaching out of the east. A number of fellow sailors offer advice on their radios, but despite all of the information offered by the guidance system itself and the helpful advice of colleagues, you realize that you cannot return to safety without any wind. So there you sit, with all of your finest technology, unable to move toward the harbor.

The Christian life is often like this. We glide out of our harbor under full sail, thrilled with delight in knowing our sins are forgiven and that we are right with God. A new love for our Redeemer fills us with gratitude, and we are eager to follow the course he has set for us in his Word. Yet as we pass into the open seas, we encounter spiritual stress. God's law, we find, provides the direction but not the power, and a panoply of spiritual technologies are available to substitute. We think that by reading this book or going to that conference or following this plan for spiritual victory or these steps for overcoming sin in our life, we can get the boat going in the right direction again.

These guides are usually neither law (i.e., God's directives) nor gospel (i.e., God's promises and acts in Christ), but helpful advice from fellow sailors. In a sense, the advice they offer is more law than gospel, since it imposes expectations and demands as conditions for success. Yet the more advice you get, the deeper your sense that you are simply dead in the water spiritually. Exhausted, you either give up and promise never to sail again or you realize that what you really need is a fresh gust of wind in your sails. That wind is always Christ in his saving office. What you really need is to be told all over again about who God is and what he has done to save you, and about the new world that awaits you because of his faithfulness to unfaithful sailors. This alone will fill your sails so that you can get safely back to the harbor when the gales blow hard.

Our whole life as Christians is a process of sailing confidently into the open seas, dying down in exhaustion, and having our sails filled again with God's precious promises. We are never at any moment simply under full sail or dead in the water, but move back and forth throughout the Christian life. This is the movement that we find in Romans 6–8, from the triumphant indicative (Rom. 6:1–11), to the moral imperatives (6:12–14), back to the indicatives (6:15–7:6), to the exhausting struggle with sin (7:7–24), back again to the triumphant indicative, "Thanks be to God through Jesus Christ our Lord!" (7:25) and the future hope awaiting us for which even now we have the Spirit as a down payment (8:1–39).

Thus the crucial point in all of this is that even in its third use (guiding rather than condemning), the law can do only what the law does. We must not think that the law drives us to Christ in the beginning (second use) and then Christ drives us back to the law for our acceptance before God in sanctification (third use). Rather, the law continues to provide us with the soundest guidance available, but apart from Christ and the indicative announcement of what he has done for us and in us, it can only lead us to either despair or self-righteousness. No less than when we first believed, we must always attribute to the gospel the power that fills our sails with gratitude, and to the law the proper course that such gratitude takes. At the beginning, in the middle, and at the end, the *gospel* "is the power of God for salvation to everyone who believes" (Rom. 1:16).

Notes

Chapter 1 The Big Idea?

1. G. E. Mendenhall, *Law and Covenant in Israel and the Ancient Near East* (Pittsburgh: The Biblical Colloquium, 1955), 24.

2. Meredith G. Kline, *The Structure of Biblical Authority* (Grand Rapids: Eerdmans, 1975), 25.

3. Ibid., 27.

4. Ibid., 57.

5. Ibid., 79.

6. Walther Eichrodt, *Theology of the Old Testament*, trans. J. A. Baker (Philadelphia: Westminster, 1951), 1:36.

7. Ibid., 37.

8. Ibid., 38, 42. Gerhard von Rad writes along similar lines, arguing that canonical saving history receives its time divisions through its covenant theology: "Focal points in the divine action now stand out in relief from parts of the history that are more epic in character, and as a result of the division perfectly definite relationships between the various epochs, of which the old summaries as yet gave no hint, are now clear. The most striking decisive moments of this kind are the making of covenants by Jahweh" (Gerhard von Rad, *Old Testament Theology*, trans. D. M. G. Stalker [New York: Harper, 1962], 1:129).

9. Eichrodt writes: "This type of popular religion, in which the divinity displays only the higher aspect of the national self-consciousness, the national 'genius,' or the mysterium in the forces of Nature peculiar to a particular country, was overcome principally by the concept of the covenant. Israel's religion is thus stamped as a 'religion of election,' using this phrase to mean that it is the divine election which makes it the exact opposite of the nature religions" (Eichrodt, *Theology of the Old Testament*, 1:43).

10. N. T. Wright, *The Climax of the Covenant: Christ and the Law in Pauline Theology* (Edinburgh: T. & T. Clark, 1991), xi.

Chapter 2 God and Foreign Relations

1. Meredith G. Kline, *The Treaty of the Great King* (Grand Rapids: Eerdmans, 1963).

2. For the connections to the ancient Near Eastern "suzerainty treaty," see ibid.

3. Mendenhall, *Law and Covenant*.

4. Delbert R. Hillers, *Covenant: The History of a Biblical Idea* (Baltimore: Johns Hopkins University Press, 1969), 30. I will appeal to this point in my discussion of the way in which the covenant holds together

the legal and relational dimensions, against the tendency in modern theologies to set them in opposition (usually in decided preference for the latter). The comparison to feudalism has enormous implications, for instance, for the common criticisms of Anselmian atonement theories, which, though open to criticism, may now be open to reassessment (cf. Kline, *Treaty of the Great King*).

   5. Viktor Korošec's *Hethitische Staatsvertraege* (Leipzig: n.p., 1931) became a major source of comparison of Hittite treaties based on a discovery in the archives of the ancient Hittite capital of treaties dating back to the fifteenth and fourteenth centuries BC (a century before conquest of Canaan). Since Delbert Hillers both updates and expands helpfully (beyond Mendenhall) on Korošec's "elements" of the suzerainty treaty, we will follow his account.

   6. Hillers, *Covenant*, 34.
   7. Ibid., 35.
   8. Ibid.
   9. Eichrodt, *Theology of the Old Testament*, 1:37.
   10. Hillers, *Covenant*, 7.
   11. Ibid., 24.
   12. . See Meredith G. Kline, *Treaty of the Great King* (Grand Rapids: Eerdmans, 1963), 65, 125
   13. Mendenhall, *Law and Covenant*, 36.
   14. Ibid., 38.
   15. Ibid., 39.
   16. Ibid., 44.
   17. Ibid., 45.
   18. Ibid., 40n38.

Chapter 3 A Tale of Two Mothers

   1. Hillers, *Covenant*, 7.
   2. Ibid., 52.
   3. Ibid., 54.
   4. Ibid., 40–41.
   5. Ibid., 41.
   6. Dennis J. McCarthy, S.J., *Treaty and Covenant: A Study in the Ancient Oriental Documents and in the Old Testament* (Rome: Biblical Institute Press, 1963), 52–55.
   7. Hillers, *Covenant*, 105.
   8. Ibid., 101–2.
   9. Ibid., 102.
   10. Ibid., 103.
   11. Ibid., 104–5.
   12. Ibid.
   13. Meredith G. Kline, *Kingdom Prologue*, vol. 3 (S. Hamilton, MA: self-published, 1986), 57.
   14. Ibid., 325.
   15. Mendenhall, *Law and Covenant*, 46.
   16. Ibid., 47. However, on the "Mark of Cain," there is good reason to recognize this as a verbal and political "mark" rather than a visible sign.
   17. Ibid., 48.
   18. "Two covenants" here is quite different from the two covenants that we have in mind. According to the view popular in mainline Protestant and Roman Catholic circles in our day, God is in covenant with the Jews in one way and in covenant with the Gentiles in another. Each covenant has its own stipulations and conditions, threats and blessings. In contrast, the New Testament makes clear that the new covenant renders the old obsolete. It is not that the church supersedes Israel, but that Israel widens to

include Gentiles. For defenses of the "two covenants" view, see Krister Stendahl, *Paul Among Jews and Gentiles* (Minneapolis: Augsburg, 1977) and Lloyd Gaston, *Paul and the Torah* (Vancouver: University of British Columbia Press, 1991).

19. Mendenhall, *Law and Covenant*, 49.

20. Hillers, *Covenant*, 110.

21. Ibid., 112.

22. Ibid., 117–18.

23. Steven L. McKenzie, *Covenant* (St. Louis: Chalice, 2000), 66.

Chapter 4 A New Covenant

1. I'm indebted to my colleague Bryan Estelle for this suggestion.

2. Hillers, *Covenant*, 124.

3. Ibid., 125.

4. Ibid., 167.

5. Ibid., 168.

6. Ibid., 146.

7. Ibid., 171.

8. *The Manual of Discipline* (1QS), v 1– vi 2, quoted in Hillers, *Covenant*, 173.

9. Hillers, *Covenant*, 187.

10. Ibid., 188.

11. McKenzie, *Covenant*, 84.

12. Geerhardus Vos, *Eschatology of the Old Testament*, ed. James T. Dennison (Phillipsburg, NJ: Presbyterian and Reformed, 2001), 130.

13. Geerhardus Vos, *Redemptive History and Biblical Interpretation: The Shorter Writings of Geerhardus Vos*, ed. Richard Gaffin Jr. (Phillipsburg, NJ: Presbyterian and Reformed 1980). "In Hebrew Scriptures the meaning 'testament' has no standing at all" (165).

14. See J. Barton Payne's *Theology of the Older Testament* (Grand Rapids: Zondervan, 1962); cf. his argument in *New Perspectives on the Old Testament* (Waco: Word, 1970).

15. O. Palmer Robertson, *The Christ of the Covenants* (Grand Rapids: Baker, 1980), 12.

16. Ibid., 139.

17. Ibid., 140.

18. Ibid., 142.

19. See Kline, *Treaty*, 41.

20. Robertson, *Christ of the Covenants*, 142n12.

21. Ibid., 146.

22. Ibid.

23. Vos, *Redemptive History and Biblical Interpretation*, 175.

24. McKenzie, *Covenant*, 6.

25. Ibid., 169–70.

26. Ibid., 170.

27. Vos, *Redemptive History and Biblical Interpretation*, 171.

28. Ibid., 163, emphasis added.

29. Ibid., 164.

30. Ibid., 178.

31. Ibid., 179.

32. Robertson, *Christ of the Covenants*, 34.

33. Vos, *Redemptive History and Biblical Interpretation*, 226.

34. Ibid., 227.

35. Ibid., 231.

36. Ibid.

37. Dennis J. McCarthy, S.J., *Old Testament Covenant: A Survey of Current Opinions* (Atlanta: John Knox, 1972), 5.

38. Ibid., 48.

39. Ibid., 50–52.

40. Ibid., 51.

Chapter 5 From Scripture to System

1. See, for example, Charles Hodge, *Systematic Theology*, vol. 2 (New York: Scribner, Armstrong and Co., 1872), 117–22, 354–70; Louis Berkhof, *Systematic Theology* (Grand Rapids: Eerdmans, 1941), 211–18, 260–88.

2. Robertson, *Christ of the Covenants*, 54.

3. Ibid.

4. Vos, *Redemptive History and Biblical Interpretation*, 245.

5. Johannes Cocceius, *Summ. Theol.* 22.1 in Heinrich Heppe, *Reformed Dogmatics*, rev. and ed. by Ernst Bizer, tr. G. T. Thompson (London: Wakeman Great Reprints, from 1950 ed.; copyright held by HarperCollins), 281; cf. Herman Witsius, 1.2.1: "The covenant of works is the agreement between God and Adam created in God's image to be the head and prince of the whole human race, by which God was promising him eternal life and felicity, should he obey all his precepts most perfectly, adding the threat of death, should he sin even in the least detail; while Adam was accepting this condition" (Heppe, *Reformed Dogmatics*, 283). The terms were that "he should by this natural holiness, righteousness and goodness possess a blessed state of life" (Eglin, *De foedere gratiae*, 2.10, Heppe, *Reformed Dogmatics*, 283). Heppe relates, "According to this the covenant of works retained the following four connections (*Wyttenbach Tent.* 2, 571): 'The act by which a first party demands something from a second is called *stipulatio*; the act by which it assigns good to it, *promissio*; while the act by which the second party takes upon itself to supply what the first had demanded is called *adstipulatio* and where it asks for the promise, *restipulatio*. Thus in any covenant there are four acts, two belonging to the party initiating the covenant, and two to that which accepts the covenant offered. In God's covenant with the first man all four covenant acts are discernible. Whereas God has demanded of man perfect keeping of the law, we have discerned the *stipulatio* in it, and whereas He promised man life in heaven and has already conferred the greatest happiness in this world, we discern the *promissio*. On the other side as long as man studied to keep God's law, *adstipulatio* was being given by him to God's demand. Had he persisted therein vigorously and non-stop, he might in the end have asked a good promise of God and so *restipulatio* would have ensued'" (295).

6. Cited in Heppe, *Reformed Dogmatics*, 283.

7. Augustine, *City of God* (bk. 16, chap. 28), ed. David Knowles, trans. Henry Bettenson (New York: Penguin Books, 1972), 688–89. He speaks of "the origin which is common to all mankind, since all have broken God's covenant in that one man in whom all sinned." There are various covenants, "But the first covenant, made with the first man, is certainly this: 'On the day you eat, you will surely die.' . . . For the covenant [curse] from the beginning is, 'You will surely die.' Now, seeing that a more explicit law was given later, and the Apostle says, 'Where there is no law, there is no law-breaking,' how can the psalm be true, where we read, 'I have counted all sinners on earth as law-breakers'? It can only be true on the assumption that those who are held bound by any sin are guilty of a breach of some law." Thus even infants are "recognized as breakers of the Law which was given in paradise." He goes on to clearly distinguish this covenant from that gracious covenant made with Abraham.

8. Irenaeus even distinguishes between "an economy of law/works" and a "Gospel covenant" ("Against Heresies," bk. 4, chap. 25, from *The Ante-Nicene Fathers*, ed. Alexander Roberts and James Donaldson (repr; Grand Rapids: Eerdmans, 1989), 5.16.3, p. 554; 4.13.1, p. 24; 4.15.1; 4.16.3 pp. 25–26.

9. Zacharias Ursinus, *Commentary on the Heidelberg Catechism* (Phillipsburg, NJ: Presbyterian and Reformed, 1985, from the 1852 Second American Edition), 1.

10. Ibid., 2–3.

11. Theodore Beza, *The Christian Faith*, trans. James Clark (East Essex, England: Focus Christian Ministries Trust, 1992), 41ff.

12. William Perkins, *The Art of Prophesying* (Edinburgh: Banner of Truth, 1996), 54.

13. Louis Berkhof, *Systematic Theology* (Grand Rapids: Eerdmans, 1941), 612: "The Law and the Gospel in the Word of God. The Churches of the Reformation from the very beginning distinguished between the law and the gospel as the two parts of the Word of God as a means of grace. This distinction was not understood to be identical with that between the Old and the New Testament, but was regarded as a distinction that applies to both Testaments. There is law and gospel in the Old Testament and there is law and gospel in the New. The law comprises everything in Scripture which is a revelation of God's will in the form of command or prohibition, while the gospel embraces everything, whether it be in the Old Testament or the New, that pertains to the work of reconciliation and that proclaims the seeking and redeeming love of God in Jesus Christ. And each one of these two parts has its own proper function in the economy of grace."

J. Van Brugen, in his *Annotations on the Heidelberg Catechism* (Neerlandia, AB: Inheritance Publications, 1998), is even clearer on this score: "The Catechism, thus, mentions the gospel and deliberately does not speak of 'the Word of God,' because the Law does not work faith. The Law (Law and gospel are the two parts of the Word which may be distinguished) judges; it does not call a person to God and does not work trust in him. The gospel does that" (170).

14. Vos, *Redemptive History and Biblical Interpretation*, 243ff.

15. Ibid., 235.

16. Ibid., 237, including n. 4.

17. Ibid., 243.

18. Ibid., 244.

19. Ibid., 245.

20. Ibid., 246.

21. John Calvin, *Institutes of the Christian Religion*, ed. John T. McNeill, trans. Ford Lewis Battles (Philadelphia: Westminster, 1960), 1.15.8: "In this integrity man by free will had the power, if he so willed, to attain eternal life. Here it would be out of place to raise the question of God's secret predestination because our present subject is not what can happen or not, but what man's nature was like. Therefore Adam could have stood if he wished, seeing that he fell solely by his own will. . . . Yet his choice of good and evil was free, and not that alone, but the highest rectitude was in his mind and will, and all the organic parts were rightly composed to obedience, until in destroying himself he corrupted his own blessings. Hence the great obscurity faced by the philosophers, for they were seeking in a ruin for a building, and in scattered fragments for a well-knit structure. They held this principle, that man would not be a rational animal unless he possessed free choice of good and evil; also it entered their minds that the distinction between virtues and vices would be obliterated if man did not order his life by his own planning. Well reasoned so far—if there had been no change in man. But since this was hidden from them, it is no wonder they mix up heaven and earth!"

22. Ibid. "By his obedience, however, Christ *truly acquired and merited* grace for us with his Father. Many passages of Scripture surely and firmly attest this. *I take it to be commonplace* that if Christ made satisfaction for sins, if he paid the penalty owed by us, if he appeased God by his obedience . . . then he *acquired* salvation for us by his righteousness, which is tantamount to *deserving it.* . . . Hence it is *absurd to set Christ's merit against God's mercy*" (2.17.1, 3, emphasis added).

The Belgic Confession says that Adam "transgressed the commandment of life" (Art. 14), terminology that was used in the emerging covenant theology (especially by Bullinger and Martyr) as interchangeable with "covenant of works." Article 22 reads: "We believe that for us to acquire the true knowledge of this great mystery the Holy Spirit kindles in our hearts a true faith that embraces Jesus Christ with *all his merits*, and makes him its own, and no longer looks for anything apart from him." Article 23: And therefore we justly say with Paul that we are justified 'by faith alone' or by faith '*apart from works*.' However, we do not mean, properly speaking, that it is faith itself that justifies us—for *faith is only the instrument by which we embrace Christ, our righteousness*. But Jesus Christ is our righteousness in making available to us *all his merits* and all *the holy works* he has done for us and in our place." It is Christ's merits, not our obedience—not even our faith, that is the ground of our salvation. In fact, if we had to appear before God relying—no matter how little—on ourselves or some other creature, then, alas, we would be swallowed up" (emphasis added).

23. This approach also rejects the stance often taken in the last half-century to set the so-called relational against the legal categories of the divine-human relationship."Covenant" is an inherently legal relationship.

24. Moreover, in the light of recent studies of ancient Near Eastern treaties, we can affirm with Meredith Kline that the arrangement in the Genesis narrative has all the elements of a covenant. Not only are the formulaic stipulations and sanctions present, as the older theologians recognized; other elements now recognized as fixtures of such covenants, such as a preamble and a historical prologue, are present as well (see Meredith Kline, *Kingdom Prologue* [vol. 1, South Hamilton, MA: self-published, 1986], 1:13). In fact, there can be little doubt that Genesis 1 and 2 constitute just such a preamble ("In the beginning God created the heavens and the earth") and narrative prologue, both contextualizing and justifying the terms of the treaty that follow. This covenant is "produced through divine words and acts of commitment and it was subject to the sanctions of ultimate divine blessing and curse.... Described in terms of varieties of international covenants familiar at the time of the writing of the Book of Genesis, the Covenant of Creation was thus a suzerain-vassal covenant plus the proposal of a special grant to the vassal for loyal service." For the distinctive elements of treaty-making, see also Klaus Baltzer, *The Covenant Formulary* (Philadelphia: Fortress, 1971).

25. While this parallel is drawn by a number of writers, it is given a thorough description and analysis in Herman Witsius (1636–1708), *The Economy of the Covenants* (Escondido, CA: The den Dulk Christian Foundation, 1990). For a more contemporary summary, see Charles Hodge, *Systematic Theology* (Grand Rapids: Eerdmans, 1946): "Besides this evangelical character which unquestionably belongs to the Mosaic covenant ['belongs to,' not 'is equivalent to'], it is presented in two other aspects in the Word of God. First, it was a national covenant with the Hebrew people. In this view the parties were God and the people of Israel; the promise was national security and land prosperity; the condition was the obedience of the people as a nation to the Mosaic law; and the mediator was Moses. In this aspect it was a legal covenant. It said 'Do this and live.' Secondly, it contained, as does also the New Testament, a renewed proclamation of the covenant of works" (2:375).

26. Peter Van Mastricht, *Theologia Theoretico-Practica*, vol. 3 (*Editio nova*, Utrecht and Amsterdam, 1725; repr., Morgan, PA: Soli Deo Gloria, 2002), xii, 23, quoted in Heppe, *Reformed Dogmatics*, 290.

27. Ibid., 289–90.

28. The Lutherans and the Reformed were agreed in rejecting the Socinian view that the image consists only in dominion and moral innocence and not wisdom, justice, and holiness (see, e.g., Francis Turretin, *Institutes of Elenetic Theology*, trans. George M. Giger, ed. James T. Dennison Jr., vol. 1 [Phillipsburg, NJ: Presbyterian and Reformed 1992], 467). And against Rome, they hold that humankind was created in a state of righteousness and not merely in a "neutral" state, and jointly affirm that this original state was natural and not a supernatural gift (see, e.g., John Theodore Mueller, *Christian Dogmatics* [St. Louis: Concordia, 1934], 206).

29. Heppe, *Reformed Dogmatics*, 290.

30. Ibid., 294.

31. Ibid., 295.

32. Ibid., 286.

33. Ibid., 287.

34. The fourth Gospel once again especially underscores the "fulfilling of all righteousness" that is central to Jesus's mission. Jesus himself uses the language of a victorious second Adam, an obedient and loyal covenant servant, who has "come . . . not to do My own will, but the will of Him who sent Me" (John 6:38 NKJV), who can say at the end of his obedient probation, "I have finished the work which You have given Me to do" (John 17:4 NKJV). The hauntingly familiar words from the cross, "It is finished" (John 19:30), take on fresh significance, as does the rending of the temple curtain, through which humanity is now invited to enter into the Sabbath land and eat from the Tree of Life.

35. Vos, *Redemptive History and Biblical Interpretation*, 193.

36. A. Cohen, *The Twelve Prophets, Hebrew Text, English Translation and Commentary* (London: Soncino, 1948), 12, quoted in Robertson, *Christ of the Covenants*, 22n3.

37. Ibid., 25.

38. Ibid., 56.

39. Ibid., 59, emphasis added.

40. Meredith G. Kline, *By Oath Consigned* (Grand Rapids: Eerdmans, 1968), 23, quoted in Robertson, *Christ of the Covenants*, 60.

41. Robertson, *Christ of the Covenants*, 61.

42. Ibid., 67.

43. Ibid., 110.

44. Ibid., 113.

45. Ibid.

46. Meredith G. Kline, "Genesis," in *New Bible Commentary Revised*, ed. D. Guthrie and J. A. Motyer (Grand Rapids: Eerdmans, 1970), 90, quoted in Robertson, *Christ of the Covenants*, 125.

47. Ibid., 124–25.

48. Ibid., 171.

49. Brevard S. Childs, *Biblical Theology of the Old and New Testaments: Theological Reflection on the Christian Bible* (Minneapolis: Fortress Press, 1993), 138.

50. Robertson, *Christ of the Covenants*, 171. This is precisely the reason adduced by E. P. Sanders (in *Paul and Palestinian Judaism* [Minneapolis: Augsburg Fortress, 1977]) and others for regarding Judaism as "covenantal nomism," in which God's grace and human faithfulness cooperate in the attainment of the blessings promised.

51. Ibid., 174.

52. Ibid., 175.

53. N. T. Wright, *The Climax of the Covenant: Christ and the Law in Pauline Theology* (Edinburgh: T. & T. Clark, 1991), 21. He cites *Genesis Rabbah* 14.6.

54. Ibid., 23.

55. Robertson, *Christ of the Covenants*, 73.

56. Karl Barth, *Gottingen Dogmatics*, ed. Hannelotte Reiffen, trans. G. W. Bromiley (Grand Rapids: Eerdmans, 1990), 1.27.3.

57. Ibid. and the introduction by Daniel L. Migliore, xxxviii.

58. Ibid., 248.

59. Rollock, *Works*, 1:52ff, quoted in Vos, *Redemptive History and Biblical Interpretation*, 249.

60. John Preston, *The New Covenant* (ed. 1639), 374–75, quoted in Vos, *Redemptive History and Biblical Interpretation*, 250.

61. Although the elaboration of covenant theology in precisely this fashion was to wait fourteen centuries, Irenaeus already reflects many of the hermeneutical motifs that underwrite it. His emphasis, for example, on "the whole economy of salvation," closely following the flow of redemptive history rather than concentrating on speculative notions (pace Origen), parallels the federal theologians. He speaks of Abraham's justification by faith prior to circumcision and his subsequent circumcision as testimony to

the fact that he was father of both Gentile and Jewish believers, who belong to one covenant in Christ. He even speaks here of the Mosaic covenant between Abraham and Christ: "But circumcision and the law of works occupied the intervening period" ("Against Heresies," bk. 4, chap. 25, in *The Ante-Nicene Fathers*, ed. Alexander Roberts and James Donaldson [repr. Grand Rapids: Eerdmans, 1989], 495–96). The promise-fulfillment pattern lays the groundwork for a covenantal hermeneutic. "If anyone, therefore, reads the Scriptures with attention, he will find in them an account of Christ, and a foreshadowing of the new calling (*vocationis*). For Christ is the treasure which was hid in the field, that is, in this world (for 'the field is the world'); but the treasure hid in the Scriptures is Christ, since He was pointed out by means of types and parables" (496). Thus, he speaks of "the typical exodus" and "our true exodus" (502). We were "in Adam" in the transgression (5.16.3, 544). Since we lost life by means of a tree, we "receive anew [this life] by the dispensation of a tree, [viz., the cross of Christ]" (5.17.3, 545). None of this is to suggest that recapitulation and federal theology are roughly equivalent, but it does represent significant areas of potential agreement. Cf. Ligon Duncan, *The Covenant Idea in Irenaeus of Lyons* (Greenville, SC: Reformed Academic Press, 1998); cf. Everett Ferguson, "The Covenant Idea in the Second Century" in *Texts and Testaments: Essays on the Early Church Fathers*, ed. W. E. March (San Antonio: Trinity University Press, 1980).

62. Vos, *Redemptive History and Biblical Interpretation*, 252.

63. Wilhelm Niesel, *Reformed Symbolics: A Comparison of Catholicism, Orthodoxy and Protestantism*, trans. David Lewis (Edinburgh and London: Oliver and Boyd, 1962), 217, 220–21. It is worth noting here that in Calvin's own reflections on the relationship of law and gospel under grace there is (as in other places) a dialectic at work. Sometimes, by "law" Calvin has in mind the old covenant generally (i.e., the Mosaic economy), in which case the pattern is shadow/promise/infancy moving toward reality/fulfillment/maturity. In other places (sometimes within the same section), "law" is the *nuda lex*, the generic category of command over against promise. Many contemporary interpreters of Calvin on this point fail to appreciate this dialectic and thus often tend toward reductionism in either separating Calvin from Luther too much or in failing to notice their different nuances. See Michael Horton, "Calvin and the Law-Gospel Hermeneutic," *Pro Ecclesia*, 6 (1997): 27–42; cf. Michael Horton, "Law, Gospel and Covenant," *Westminster Theological Journal*, 64, no. 2 (2002), 279–87.

64. Vos, *Redemptive History and Biblical Interpretation*, 254.

65. Ibid., 255.

66. Ibid., 256. In Lutheran dogmatics "everything depends on this justification, which is losable, so that the believer only gets to see a little of the glory of grace and lives for the day, so to speak. The covenantal outlook is the reverse. One is first united to Christ, the Mediator of the covenant, by a mystical union, which finds its conscious recognition in faith. By this union with Christ all that is in Christ is simultaneously given."

Chapter 6 Providence and Covenant

1. Horace Bushnell quoted by Josiah Strong, "Our Country," in William G. McLoughlin, ed., *The American Evangelicals, 1800–1900: An Anthology* (Gloucester, MA: Peter Smith, 1976), 196.

2. Ibid.

3. D. L. Moody quoted in George M. Marsden, *Fundamentalism and American Culture* (New York: Oxford University Press, 1980), 38.

4. Augustine, *City of God*, quoted in Vernon J. Bourke, ed., *The Essential Augustine* (Indianapolis: Hacket, 1983), 201.

5. Ibid., 222.

6. Ibid., 208.

7. Calvin, *Institutes*, 2.2.15.

8. Ibid., 4.20.1–2.

9. Ibid.

10. Calvin, *Institutes*, 4.20.16.

11. Ibid.

Chapter 7 The Covenant People

1. This remains the crucial difference between covenant theology and even what has come to be called "progressive dispensationalism." See Robert Saucy, *The Case for Progressive Dispensationalism* (Grand Rapids: Zondervan, 1993).

2. See Stendahl and Gaston note above (chap. 3, note 18).

3. Kline, *Structure of Biblical Authority*, 269.

4. Ibid., 272.

5. Excerpt from the treaty of Tudhaliyas IV with Ulmi-Teshub, quoted in Kline, *Structure of Biblical Authority*, 29.

6. Kline, *Structure of Biblical Authority*, 14. This volume explores the relationship of canon and covenant.

7. Kline, *Structure of Biblical Authority*, 14.

8. McKenzie, *Covenant*, 273.

9. Ibid., 274.

Chapter 8 Signs and Seals of the Covenant

1. Vos, *Redemptive History and Biblical Interpretation*, 137.

2. James Hastings, ed., *Encyclopedia of Religion and Ethics* (New York: Scribner, n.d.), 2:601.

3. Kline, *Structure of Biblical Authority*, 16.

4. McCarthy, *Treaty and Covenant*, 195.

5. Robertson, *Christ of the Covenants*, 4.

6. Ibid., 8.

7. Ibid., 10–11.

8. Kline, *Structure of Biblical Authority*, 43–44.

9. Ibid., 45.

10. Ibid.

11. Ibid., 47.

12. Ibid., 49.

13. Ibid., 51.

14. Ibid., 54.

15. Ibid., 56–57.

16. Ibid., 57.

17. Ibid., 58–59.

18. Ibid., 60.

19. Ibid.

20. Ibid., 64.

21. Ibid., 66–67.

22. Ibid., 68.

23. Ibid.

24. Ibid., 70.

25. Ibid., 74.

26. Ibid., 77.

27. Herman Ridderbos, *Paul: An Outline of His Theology*, tr. John R. deWitt (Grand Rapids: Eerdmans, 1975), 397.

28. Ibid., 398.

29. Ibid., 399.
30. Ibid., 400.
31. Ibid., 408.
32. Ibid., 409.
33. Ibid.
34. Ibid., 411.
35. Karl Deddens, *Where Everything Points to Him*, trans. Theodore Plantinga (Neerlandia, AB: Inheritance, 1993), 93.
36. Ibid., 91.
37. Ibid., 92.
38. Ridderbos, *Paul*, 426.
39. Ibid., 427.
40. John Murray, *Collected Writings* (Edinburgh: Banner of Truth, 1977), 2:368–69.
41. John Calvin, *Commentary on a Harmony of the Evangelists*, trans. William Pringle, reprint (Grand Rapids: Baker, 1996), 3:206.
42. Ibid., 207, 209, emphasis added.
43. Ibid., 210.
44. Ibid., 211.
45. Ibid., 213.
46. Murray, *Collected Writings*, 379.
47. Calvin, *Commentary*, 214.
48. Ibid.
49. Ibid., 215.
50. Ibid.
51. Murray, *Collected Writings*, 368.
52. Ibid., 375.
53. Johannes Wollebius, in *Reformed Dogmatics: J. Wollebius, G. Voetius, F. Turretin*, trans and ed. John W. Beardslee III (New York: Oxford University Press, 1965), 134.
54. Belgic Confession, Art. 33, *Ecumenical Creeds and Reformed Confessions* (Grand Rapids: CRC Publications 1988), 111.
55. Beza, *Christian Faith*, 50–67.
56. Ibid.
57. A. A. Hodge, *Evangelical Theology: A Course of Popular Lectures* (Edinburgh: Banner of Truth, 1976), 355.
58. Ibid., 356.
59. Ridderbos, *Paul*, 422.
60. Ibid., 423.
61. Geerhardus Vos, *Redemptive History and Interpretation*, 125.

Chapter 9 New Covenant Obedience

1. Kline, *By Oath Consigned*, 19–20.
2. Ibid., 20.
3. Calvin, *Institutes*, 2.6.7, quoted in Kline, *By Oath Consigned*, 22.
4. Ibid., 23.
5. David F. Wright, book review of Elise Anne McKee, ed., *John Calvin: Writings on Pastoral Piety*, in *The Bulletin of the Institute for Reformed Theology* 4, no. 2 (Fall 2004): 9.
6. Formula of Concord, Epitome, Art 6, in *The Book of Concord: The Confessions of the Evangelical Lutheran Church*, trans. and ed. Theodore G. Tappert (Philadelphia: Fortress, 1959), 479–81.
7. John Murray, *Principles of Conduct* (Grand Rapids: Eerdmans, 1957), 181f.

Michael Horton (Ph.D., University of Coventry and Wycliffe Hall, Oxford) is professor of apologetics and theology at Westminster Seminary California. He is also editor-in-chief of *Modern Reformation* magazine, co-host of *The White Horse Inn*, a nationally syndicated radio program, and the author of numerous articles and books, including *A Better Way: Rediscovering the Drama of God-Centered Worship* and *Putting Amazing Back into Grace: Embracing the Heart of the Gospel.* A minister in the United Reformed Churches in North America (URCNA), Horton has served two churches in Southern California and resides with his wife, Lisa, and their four children in Escondido, California.